COUNSELING the INVOLUNTARY and RESISTANT CLIENT

KITTITAS COUNTY JUVENILE SERVICES
Room 211 County Courthouse
Ellensburg, WA 98926
(509) 962-6811 ext. 310

by George A. Harris, Ph.D.
and
David Watkins, Ph.D.

American Correctional Association
4321 Hartwick Road
Suite L-208
College Park, MD 20740
(301) 699-7600

Editor: Elizabeth Watts
Typesetter: Marilyn C. White
Graphic Artist: Nancy LaFontaine
Cover design and illustrations: Alonzo L. Winfield III

Copyright © 1987 by the American Correctional Association.
All rights reserved.

The reproduction, distribution, and inclusion in other publications of materials in this book is prohibited without prior written permission from the American Correctional Association.

ISBN 0-942974-87-5
Printed in the United States of America

Acknowledgements

Thanks to Ben Coates, Dr. Elizabeth Campbell, Dr. Rod Goodyear, Mary Lindsay, M.S.W., Dr. Karl Menninger, Dr. Gene Pekarik, and Dr. Virginia Pruitt for many helpful suggestions with the manuscript, and to Audrey Bolton, Mary Falter, and LeAnn Staub for patiently typing it. Special appreciation to Dr. Wallace Verburg for use of the checklist in Chapter 9 and to Katherine Kent, M.S., whose style has influenced many sections of the book too numerous to cite and document. Thanks also to Plenum Press and Dr. M. F. Basch, M.D., for permission to quote from *Resistance—Psychodynamic and Behavioral Approaches*. Initial financial support for the development of this manuscript was given by the Washburn University of Topeka faculty research grant program.

This book is dedicated to our children; Jennifer Harris, and Luke and Claire Watkins; and to our parents, the late Charles and Dorothy Harris and Kay and David Watkins.

TABLE OF CONTENTS

Foreword vi

Preface vii

Chapter 1 • Introduction 1

Chapter 2 • Theory and the Involuntary Client 5

Chapter 3 • Ethical and Legal Issues and the
Involuntary Client 9

Chapter 4 • Defining Resistance 15
   Involuntariness and resistance 16
   The necessity of resistance 17
   An overview of resistance in clinical work 17
      Resistance predicted by the way people learn 19
      Is the resistance conscious or willful? 20
      Resistance as a function of the aim of counseling 22
      Resistance and limitation of choice 24
      Resistance as a function of the amount of change
         needed 24
      Family systems and resistance 25

Chapter 5 • Inhibitors and Facilitators of
Communication 29
   The inhibitors 30
      Competing demands for time 30
      Etiquette 30
      Trauma 31
      Cultural differences 31
   The facilitators 32
      Fulfilling expectations 32
      Sympathetic understanding 32
      New experience 33
      Need for meaning 33

Chapter 6 • Resistance in Beginning Sessions 35
   When clients will not talk 36
      Identifying reasons for not talking 37
      Consequences for failure to participate 39
      Giving away power and other ways to break the
         initial impasse 41
   How to develop empathy with involuntary clients 42

When clients deny the value of counseling 46
Other problems of denial 49
Premature termination 50
Resistance to initiating therapy: A case in point 51

Chapter 7 • Principles of Working with Involuntary Clients 59
Providing structure: Setting expectations 60
Maximizing choice, minimizing demand 61
Saving face 62
Ignoring resistance or not taking the bait 62
Creating optimum anxiety to stimulate self-examination 63
Timing interventions for critical moments 65
Piquing curiosity 65
Identifying positive intent 66
Using nonverbal techniques 67
Capitalizing on various styles of learning and change 67

Chapter 8 • Stages of Accessibility in Institutional Treatment 71
Theory vs. reality in institutional treatment 72
A correctional model 74
A psychodynamic hospital model 76

Chapter 9 • Typologies and Techniques 79
The verbal attacker 81
Common ploys of the attacker 82
The defender 86
Common ploys of the defender 86
The fogger 91
Common ploys of the fogger 91

Chapter 10 • Special Issues 95
Self-awareness issues 96
Problems of alliances in institutions 97
Dealing with physically aggressive clients 100
Substance abuse counseling 102
Dealing with antisocial clients 103

Chapter 11 • Conclusion 105

Bibliography 108

Foreword

It is relatively easy to work with people who wish to make some substantive changes in their lives. In fact, many therapists believe that time shouldn't be wasted on people who are reluctant to look at themselves. Well, that may govern the world of voluntary counseling, but it certainly doesn't apply where clients are ordered to receive therapy; when the client does not want to be helped but only shows up to see the "shrink" because the court or other authority requires it.

With today's increasing use of correctional resources, working with more and more resistant clients or inmates is a given. There are more than 3 million people in the United States under some form of correctional supervision, and the communities from which they come expect them to change from a life of crime to one of decent, hard-working citizenry. It is a very difficult situation to change, and our level of expectation tends to be much higher than reality.

The world of counseling the involuntary or resistant client, probationer, parolee, or inmate is not any easy one and never will be. Thousands of mental health professionals and counselors go to work every day wondering "why bother?" Many counselors are in distress over their role in dealing with these people. If the client shows up, something should happen, but if the client won't participate, how can it?

George A. Harris and David Watkins offer no panacea, but they do offer a great deal of insight. They examine moral, legal, and ethical problems, tell how to break through the defense mechanisms of involuntary and resistant clients, and point out what is necessary to understand about them. As is true in many areas of working with people, if we understand their dynamics and motivations, we can determine what the change agent can and cannot do.

There are few other books that attempt to address this subject. For correctional professionals who must work with people sent or released to them, this book will be invaluable. But meeting the resistant client is not only reserved for those working in correctional programs. The techniques outlined in *Counseling the Involuntary and Resistant Client* can be used by counselors in public schools, hospitals, and mental health clinics. In fact, after reading it, I concluded that parents of teenagers struggling to help their children grow up can benefit by understanding the concepts Harris and Watkins discuss. This soon-to-be classic should be required reading for all active counselors, therapists, and students of counseling techniques.

Anthony P. Travisono
Executive Director

Preface

When the practice of counseling and psychotherapy was in its infancy in the early part of this century, few people imagined that a doctor could cure mysterious ailments through talk about dreams, childhood experiences, and fantasies. For many it was an amazing discovery to find that the unconscious could have such profound effects on behavior and physical well-being. The application of therapy was at first limited to a very select group: patients who voluntarily sought private treatment. At that time, mental institutions did not employ analysts; prisons did not have psychologists; and no judge would have thought to consult a psychiatrist before pronouncing sentence on those who were criminally convicted. But things have changed remarkably in a few decades.

With the base of knowledge about the causes of human behavior growing, nonmedical therapists began offering their services for newly perceived or newly developed social problems. Moreover, the use of psychological concepts has not been restricted to psychiatrists, psychologists, and social workers. Today, probation and parole officers, psychiatric paraprofessionals, court service workers, juvenile guardians and caretakers, and counselors with a variety of academic backgrounds are assigned to work with clients who would never have been deemed candidates for therapy, counseling, psychological treatment, or public supervision twenty years ago.

Many of these clients are placed in detention or coerced into treatment by courts and social welfare agencies. In the modern era, unlike any previous era, counselors and therapists are faced with involuntary, unwilling clients. Reluctance to enter treatment is probably the most important and pervasive issue facing today's change agent in hundreds of settings. The self-referred client is for many therapists the exception rather than the rule.

Counselors in a variety of settings work with involuntary clients: in correctional programs, schools, and state mental institutions that work with detained or confined clients. Problems of substance abuse, domestic violence, and child abuse are increasingly a concern, and state welfare services often require counseling as an alternative to court. But counselors in private practice are increasingly sent court-ordered referrals: people who avoid prosecution or imprisonment by agreeing to treatment. Marriage and family counselors often see couples or families in which not all parties are enthusiastic about being in treatment. Teachers work with students who are rebellious and reluctant to learn and change.

This book aims to provide basic principles and recommendations for those counselors who have already had basic training in helping relationships, but find themselves frustrated by the gap between academic theory and practice when it comes to dealing with the involuntary and resistant client.

This book does not pertain to medically related disorders or to the medical management of psychiatric patients. We believe that the majority of involuntary clients have no psychological dysfunctions for which medical treatment is effective. Though many involuntary clients are diagnosable as having personality disorders, our focus is not on treating those disorders but on counseling the wide variety of people who are coerced into treatment for various problems.

After an introduction to the problem of the involuntary and resistant client and a review of theory, legal and ethical considerations will be reviewed. We will then define resistance and give examples of behaviors commonly called resistant.

A brief overview of resistance is presented as it is conceptualized by various approaches, e.g., psychoanalytic, behavioral, family systems. This will be followed by a discussion of principles and techniques for managing and working with involuntary clients, particularly those in institutional settings. Some of the principles discussed derive from recognized theories and assumptions about human behavior. Others are more atheoretical, accumulated from our practice and clinical experience. The discussion throughout will be aimed at the professional working "in the trenches" with clients who are caught up in a therapeutic change process at someone else's request, and pose special problems in counseling because of their resistance to treatment.

1
Introduction

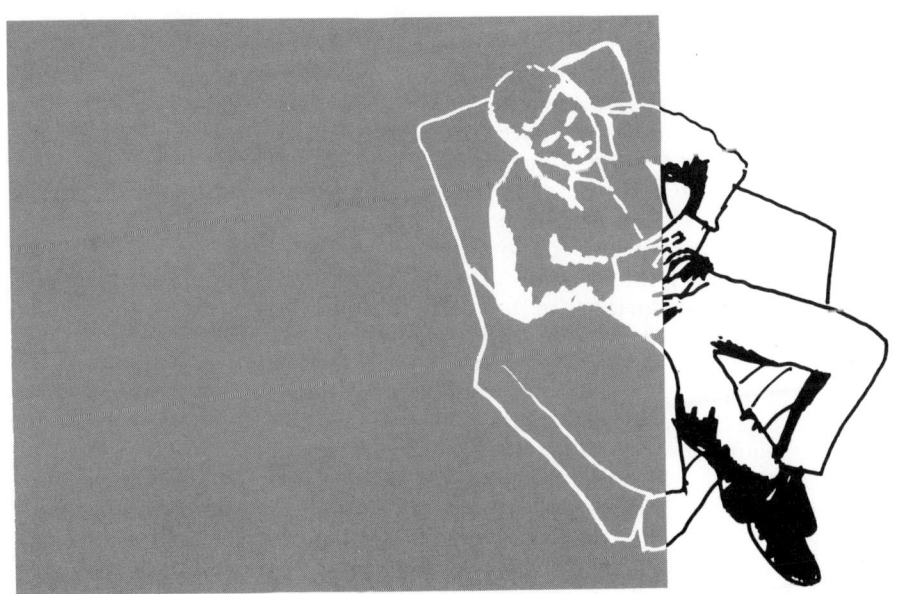

Chapter One

Sam listened intently and felt a sense of relief when the judge deferred prosecution on the condition that he get counseling. Not that he needed head shrinking, Sam thought, but the alternative was probably jail. "Twelve sessions and I'm free," he mused. "I can get through twelve sessions; no problem."

Sam's lawyer also thought the diversion program was a good deal and said so. The counselor in the court services division needed only to report to the judge that Sam had successfully completed the required sessions. So with the lawyer's help, Sam arranged for his first appointment a week away.

As the time for the first meeting approached, Sam began to feel angry at the whole mess. His wife still would not see him. He had left messages for her at the battered women's shelter, but she never returned his calls. He was sure the staff people were not giving her the messages; they were busybodies interfering where they did not belong. If they had kept their noses out of it, he would not have been dragged out of his own house like a criminal. Whose business was it if he and his wife had a fight? What right did anyone have to tell him what he could and could not do in his own home? Besides, the two of them could have worked it out themselves if they had been left alone. Anyway, Sam thought, she'd provoked him and goaded him until he couldn't stand it anymore, and now he was paying the price. As angry as he was at her, he knew he wanted her back, and he sometimes felt depressed and angry enough to kill himself—and her if she would not cooperate.

Sam arrived for his initial counseling session barely on time. He had to rush to get there because he was on his lunch hour. He had almost lost his job when he was arrested and detained, and he could not afford any more time off. He barely had time to get seated in the waiting room when a man about the age of his younger brother called his name.

"Hi, I'm Jeff. Why don't you grab a cup of coffee and come on in."

Sam and Jeff walked down the hall to a small, tile-floored room with a couple of easy chairs and a few sick-looking plants. Jeff motioned to a chair and asked Sam to have a seat.

"Sam, I know a little about your situation from the court record and I imagine you're less than thrilled about having to come here, even though you chose this over prosecution. Is that right?"

"Yes," Sam responded cautiously. He had figured this counselor was going to start by lecturing him for a while about wife-beating, so the beginning was a bit of a surprise, and it took a little wind out of his sails. Jeff then asked Sam to talk a little about what he wanted to accomplish in counseling, a request that also took Sam off guard.

Frankly, Sam told Jeff, he didn't know of anything he needed to accomplish except to get his wife back.

"I see," Jeff said. "You mean there's nothing about yourself you really need to change? You're a perfect human being caught in an unfair situation?"

Sam started to become a little hot under the collar. Who was this sar-

castic jerk anyway? "I never said I was perfect," he replied. "But what I need, you can't give me unless you can talk my wife into letting me come home."
"I wouldn't if I could," Jeff said. "Anyway, I imagine she'd tell me you have to change first."
"Change what?" Sam asked angrily.
"Listen, Sam, please don't be mad at me. I didn't file the charges against you, and I didn't order you here. I just wanted to know if you saw anything you wanted to talk about while you're in counseling."
"What good will it do to come in here and yak about it? That's not going to get my wife back," Sam retorted. He was still angry, but he also recognized that blaming the counselor would be unreasonable.
"You don't think there's anything you might learn that would help you get along with your wife better? If so, you're a rare person; almost everybody could use a little help on that score," Jeff said.
"Sure, I'm human. I just don't think I'm the only one at fault in this deal. She ought to be in counseling too, if getting along better is what we're trying to do."
"I didn't say you were the only one at fault," Jeff answered. "I didn't say anyone was at fault. Maybe your wife should be here, but she's not. So the question is, do you want to see if there's anything you and I can do in the next twelve weeks to help you get along better with her? I can't guarantee we'll find anything, and if we do, I can't guarantee she'll let you move home. But that's all we can do. You want to try?"
"I guess so," Sam said, weary and depressed.
Jeff knew Sam wasn't going to be an easy client. He realized that Sam had not chosen counseling freely. Sam was a typical reluctant client who did not perceive his responsibility for his plight; he blamed others for it. But Jeff knew he could not admonish him until Sam admitted his responsibility. In fact, talking about blame on anyone's part is usually futile.
Jeff also knew that Sam, like most people, would dislike being told what to do. Everyone likes to feel as if choices exist, and we all resent those who restrict our choices. So Jeff explicitly disassociated himself from the coercion behind Sam's being there without criticizing the judge, the police, or Sam's wife, because Jeff knew Sam would rebel against him if he were linked with the court order.
Sam also made it clear to Jeff that he doubted whether talk would do much good. Jeff knew that people who felt this way seldom asked for counseling, which, after all, is just talk. Jeff knew there was no way to prove the worth of counseling to Sam, who would gain faith in the counseling process only through success with it. But at the least, Jeff wanted to elicit Sam's cooperation to begin, if only because it was the only hope that Sam had.
Sam had not elected counseling, and this situation created many roadblocks to getting counseling started. But Jeff also knew that even when these roadblocks were overcome, Sam would still resist changing. The form of his resistance could only be imagined at this first session. Would he feel less a man if he could not dominate his wife? Did he feel the need to control people in general, and would he resist giving up the advantages of that

way of living for the advantages of more equal, reciprocal relationships? Would his wife find the changes in him satisfying and sufficient enough to warrant a new start, and would she respond to him without blaming him only for their past problems?

Each couple—each person—is different. Even people who ask for help resist it, and Jeff knew that people who are forced into counseling pose special obstacles as well as unique and fascinating challenges. Jeff realized that if he had any hope of helping Sam, he would need to use all his understanding of change and resistance to change. Jeff would need to understand the special agony of the person who is floundering in deep water but fights off the lifeguard who is trying to help.

2

Theory and the Involuntary Client

Chapter Two

As knowledge of human behavior expanded, the art of psychotherapy evolved. Since Freud's time, a proliferation of human problems has been subjected to the methods and concepts developed from the study of psychology. Today, mental health professionals treat not only problems of neurotic adjustment, but also difficulties of delinquency and criminal behavior, sexual misconduct, and a host of other disorders. Although Freud's influence has been profound, his conceptualization of human behavior has not gone unchallenged. Newer approaches, such as behaviorism and family systems theories, seek to redefine normal and abnormal behavior and their causes.

In the last decade, some writers have argued that a fundamental change has occurred in the way most people relate to their social environment. Lasch (1978), for example, wrote about the culture of narcissism, arguing that individuals have become too focused on self and implying that their sense of responsibility and contribution to others has decreased. If this is true, then do the problems encountered in counseling today reflect this change? Does this new breed of client care about others? Can they be influenced to adapt their behavior through awareness of its effect on others? Can they feel guilt and anxiety about failing to live up to societal expectations? Can they be motivated to change by the same techniques used to help other people who feel anxiety when they fail at life's tasks? Do these new clients seek counseling only when forced into it by external pressures? Certainly, antisocial behavior is an age-old problem, but is irresponsibility on the rise because of cultural changes, or are these problems becoming more prominent because of increased media attention? There are no obvious answers to these questions, but it does appear that today there are many clients who reluctantly enter treatment not at their own volition but at the request of someone else.

Many psychological theories of behavior have their origins in a theorist's clinical experience. Freud, for example, developed psychoanalytic theory not from formal experimentation, but from his clinical practice. Today, however, theories developed from work with one population are being applied to clients, groups, and problems not previously seen in clinical practice. The question is whether techniques that evolved and were used, for example, in a college counseling center will be equally effective in a prison or drug treatment program. Are there important differences in the setting or the type of people encountered that will require changes in approach? Little has been written about the problems of adapting psychological theories to clients who are involuntary and reluctant to participate in a change process.

Counselors and therapists have not failed to notice that clients resist treatment, often paradoxically, at the same time that their expressions of desire to change are most adamant. In fact, the study of resistance is regarded by psychoanalytic theorists as of crucial and central importance. Menninger (1958), in describing the theory of psychoanalysis, devoted a full chapter to the types of resistance encountered as the patient regresses to display primitive, childlike behavior during therapy, then begins to rebound, showing more mature, functional methods of coping.

Menninger also likened the process of psychoanalysis to a business contract in which the buyer (patient) purchases something of value (therapy) from the seller (analyst). He noted that patients may not understand exactly what they are buying; they enter the agreement thinking they are buying relief from and help with their symptoms. But what they get does not satisfy them at first, because they have unrealistic expectations about what others should and can do for them and how others should gratify their needs for approval and attention. As therapy progresses, patients become frustrated and angry and resist forming adult behaviors and views. Their particular method of resistance depends on what psychological defenses they typically use to avoid anxiety as they gain awareness of themselves.

Menninger's analogy between the therapeutic contract and a business contract helps us understand the problem of the involuntary client who, like an uninterested customer, sees no value in the product being sold. The counselor must decide how and whether to "sell" the product to gain the client's cooperation in the process. Counseling seldom delivers tangible gain, but that is precisely what the client is looking for. An inmate, for example, would see value in counseling if it helped to gain early release from prison, but counselors cannot promise such a thing. The value of counseling is seldom obvious or easily explainable to the client, who generally must buy the product trusting the professional to do good work. Only after treatment is completed—or at least well under way—does the client begin to understand what is being bought. Thus, the involuntary client resists treatment like the consumer resists buying unwanted products and services. But unlike the normal consumer, the involuntary client often feels coerced into buying because the consequence of not buying is undesirable; a Hobson's choice, the lesser of two evils.

It is important then to determine how traditional theories developed with voluntary clients will apply to those who are coerced, and if they will apply at all. Time-honored methods must be reevaluated to assess their effectiveness. The reluctant client, an involuntary participant in counseling, is likely to resist treatment in all the ways that the voluntary client might, but the coerced entry into counseling compounds the resistance and adds new dimensions to the beginning of the counseling process.

Although many theories have sought to explain human behavior, no single theory has emerged to offer a comprehensive explanation and no one treatment approach has proven entirely effective. The various theorists view resistance through many kinds of lenses. Freudians conceptualize resistance as the manifestation of the client's crucial, unconscious defense mechanism. Cognitive behavioral theorists attribute recalcitrance to inadequate therapy (Lazarus and Fay, 1982). But treatment approaches that are effective in a traditional counselor/patient relationship may be cumbersome or simply unworkable for modern helping relationships, such as parole officers paid by the state to both counsel and police clients. So although resistance is a recognized phenomenon in most therapeutic approaches, the nature and meaning of resistance is not agreed upon and has not been sufficiently reexamined as the net of social service programs has expanded to include an increasingly diverse client group in new and different contexts.

It could be argued that treatment specialists themselves have resisted abandoning old theories that do not fit new problems and situations. For example, there are very few treatment approaches developed for use specifically with delinquents and criminals. Reality therapy (Glasser, 1965) perhaps fits this description. Yochelson and Samenow's treatment model in *The Criminal Personality* (1976, 1977) is probably the most comprehensive study available of an antisocial client group. The diversity of approaches for working with reluctant clients may be limited because professionals with the most training, and presumably the greatest ability to treat difficult and reluctant clients, are themselves reluctant to work with such clients. Salaries for institutional workers are generally low, and as counselors enhance their professional credentials, they tend to leave institutions to work with more financially rewarding clients.

Literally thousands of mental health workers today are treating clients who came to treatment by different referral routes and for different reasons than those clients whose cases helped shape the writing of most modern psychological theorists. While these theories and techniques are not unusable, they should be reviewed to determine their practical application to working with involuntary and resistant clients. Most agency and institutional counselors do not have the luxury of excessive theorizing; they need practical suggestions. But since practice is grounded in theory, it is hoped that an exploration of ideas will stimulate greater theoretical understanding, which, along with the practical suggestions offered, can be integrated to provide a balanced approach to clinical practice.

3

Ethical and Legal Issues and the Involuntary Client

Chapter Three

The ethical issues involved in counseling involuntary clients should be considered prior to examining actual techniques. After all, what is the point of learning to do something if it shouldn't be done at all? The discussion that follows covers only a sample of the problems that are posed by working with the involuntary client. Many ethical dilemmas are best seen when techniques themselves are being examined, so there will also be comments throughout the text about such problems. At a minimum, we hope some exploration of the topic will spur readers to think about the issues.

Merely raising the question of what is and is not ethical seems to presume that certain human characteristics exist. Concern and respect for human rights implies a belief in the person as something more than mere protoplasm reacting to stimuli. Besides the obvious protection from physical harm, humans are presumed to have the right to be protected from psychological harm, such as could come from coerced treatment and its pressures. Kittrie (1971) recognized the right of society to mandate treatment under certain circumstances, such as when the individual presents a clear and present danger to others, but generally speaking, the right of the person to refuse treatment is recognized.

Why is it that people are presumed to have the right to refuse treatment? Our culture places a high value on the existence of the human will, which makes possible freedom of choice. It is interesting that so many psychological theories pay little attention to the human will and thus overlook the effects that restrictions of choice have on people. Behavioral theory, for example, presumes that behavior is a function of prior reinforcement experiences and so does not acknowledge the role of individual choice in a person's behavior. But in our legal system, there is definite recognition of and respect for the individual's right to choose.

Some texts on counseling assert that the counseling relationship can only take place with the mutual consent of the individuals involved (Shertzer and Stone, 1974). We believe this is the ideal relationship but one seldom found. Many clients are led into treatment, even when they present no clear and present danger to anyone, by parents, spouses, or legal authorities. Haley (1963) commented on the coerced nature of almost all counseling relationships, and it is psychologically naive to pretend that even clients who seek therapy voluntarily aren't ambivalent about the prospect of changing. Perhaps it is simplistic to think of clients as either voluntary or involuntary; it would be more accurate to recognize the conflict the person experiences as he or she is faced with entering therapy.

Let us take a specific case. A teenage boy is brought to counseling against his will by his parents, who are concerned about his drug use. The boy clearly states he doesn't want to come to counseling, yet just as clearly (to the counselor) reveals an anxiety about his life's direction; an anxiety that he admits he wishes were not there. The teenager rejects counseling, perhaps because he is unable to "choose" to work on a problem that he (perhaps unconsciously) fears he will either be unable to solve or that will lead to even greater problems if it is solved (such as the responsibilities of adulthood). Is it ethical to dismiss this boy as unwilling to undergo treatment because he says that's how he feels? Even if it means he will spiral into deeper and deeper substance abuse? We think not.

The purpose of this book is to explore ways to increase the client's voluntary cooperation and to get the person to acknowledge that such cooperation is in his or her best interest. If those efforts to gain cooperation are not harmful, then should the counselor be concerned about treating clients against their will? The techniques discussed in this book can be likened to a low pressure sales pitch. If they work, fine, if they do not, no harm done.

There is evidence that forced treatment, however, can do harm. A report by the National Institute for Juvenile Justice and Delinquency Protection (1983) stated that forced treatment was a precursor to violence in juvenile institutions and that voluntary choice was necessary to encourage clients to take ownership in their therapeutic program. It is important, however, not to expect troubled clients to enthusiastically endorse treatment. Counselors should expect to have to go slowly in gaining the cooperation generally thought necessary for effective treatment.

Counseling the involuntary client frequently raises issues regarding invasion of privacy, manipulation, loyalty, confidentiality, and obligations to report. To what extent should a counselor pry into the life of someone who protests such investigation? Should a counselor try to influence clients in ways beyond their awareness? When a client is referred by a third party, what are the counselor's obligations to the referral source or to the agency that pays the bill? What should the counselor do if clients report illegal activity or threaten harm to others? How clearly should the involuntary client understand the nature of treatment before consenting to it?

It would be naive to act as though the involuntary client were no different from other clients with regard to the counselor/client relationship. For example, there clearly are divisions of loyalty when a counselor's salary is paid by a correctional institution to counsel inmates (Berman and Segal, 1982). The American Psychological Association report on ethics of psychologists in the criminal justice system (1978) addressed at least some of the issues and is essential reading. However, social workers, ministers, school counselors, probation officers, and psychiatrists may not only hold different ethical perspectives but also may be subject to varying legal requirements and protections. There may be privileged communication for one professional group in a given state but not for another. Many states require professions to report suspected child abuse, and case law requires that threats of harm should be reported immediately to protect the person threatened (Van Hoose and Kottler, 1985.) The counselor may also be expected to take measures to protect the intended victim, such as attempting to achieve a commitment of self-control from the client. Given these considerations, here are a few preliminary recommendations that may help counselors remain legally protected:

1. Counselors should know the case law in their jurisdiction and should read the code of ethics for their profession.

The ethical standards of different disciplines may imply the existence of autonomy, which the law precludes. Or it may be discovered that actual proceedings seem not to follow ethical criteria as written. For example, although counselors may believe they should have privileged communication with their client, their employer may demand information, despite the code of ethics. Judges, too, may not abide by the standards of the profession. Witness the recent cases of journalists sentenced to jail for refusing to divulge sources of information. It is important to remember that things do not always work as they are supposed to or as they are articulated on paper.

Certain types of therapy, such as severe aversive conditioning, have generally been prohibited for incarcerated clients—even those who volunteer—because there is no such thing as voluntary choice when participation could lead to early release or other material advantage. Highly confrontive verbal techniques, such as hot seats, could also be judged inappropriate and intrusive. If in doubt about a particular technique, clearance from superiors should be requested in writing. (It is always a good idea to have supervision or consultation on difficult cases.) Then, activities should be documented plainly.

2. Clients should be advised in advance about issues of confidentiality. If clients are told in advance what may be divulged, then they have little room for complaint. Simple, direct statements are best. There is no reason to make a big fuss about it. In most cases, the client is not a bit bothered by the explanation and will not cooperate any the less for it. Paradoxically, many people are suspicious when given broad guarantees about the uniqueness and protections of the counselor/client relationship and become more trusting when told what the limits are.

3. Elementary records should be kept, and it should be assumed they could be read by judges and attorneys. Records may be subpoenaed, so it is wise to avoid professional jargon that is difficult to explain to lay people. If counselors are subpoenaed and asked to break confidentiality, they might try to request that their testimony be heard in chambers rather than in an open courtroom. The request may or may not be granted but is worth a try.

4. Clients should be informed about the treatment procedure being used and its possible side effects. As noted previously, it is not always easy to explain treatment to clients. Counselors almost always form opinions and hypotheses about new clients and their problems that are better left unexplained to clients initially. Alternative treatment procedures should also be explained, and clients should be asked to sign consent forms for any release of information and for any controversial treatment technique.

Another issue to consider in working with involuntary clients is the extent to which counselors should manipulate and persuade their clients. At what point does counseling become like mind control? Are some techniques too much like a "hard sell?" Can clients ever be coerced into doing something against their will? How do we decide whether a technique is being used solely or mainly for the client's welfare? Can clients be tricked into doing things they will later regret? How much anxiety or emotional pain should counselors be allowed to arouse through confrontation?

The problem of deciding what is unethical manipulation and what is legitimate persuasion in therapy is complex. The ends do not always justify the means, but there may be a continuum of reasonableness. Providing information is hard to question ethically. Explaining to clients how a particular agency works and what resources are available are unequivocally ethical interventions. Similarly, active listening is not likely to be questioned as unethical. Helping clients gain awareness of options and choices is permissible, even if the client did not fully realize that this objective was the intent of counseling.

Counseling designed to persuade a client to take a particular course of action is more likely to be criticized, even if the course of action is in itself good. This is because freedom of choice has such high value in our society. For example, a pedophile might be behaviorally conditioned against his will to be repelled at the sight of a child. This behavioral approach may be questioned on ethical grounds, while counseling that helps the rapist discern other ways to manage his aggression would be considered proper, even if the client did not originally express a desire to learn about other aways of managing his aggression.

Emotional persuasion is more likely to be perceived as unfair than logical reasoning. A client may be persuaded to participate in some activity through a "bandwagon" technique, that is, by being told that all of his or her friends are going to do it too. However, explaining the nature of the activity and defining its advantages and disadvantages may be perceived as fostering a greater degree of choice and independence than emotional persuasion.

Although paradoxical techniques may be viewed by some as too tricky and domineering, they are often effective at instigating change. In one group session, for example, a counselor instructed a constantly complaining client to be sure to find three things during the session to "whine" about. Being told to complain apparently took the fun of rebellion out of the behavior, so the client stopped. The rebelliousness was channeled constructively.

Rollo May (1969) stated that all protest was only half-formed will and that the paradox of therapy was that all clients are seeking help to become more autonomous. The involuntary client, however, has not formulated to himself the request to be "therapized," and so has not consented to being "tricked" by paradoxical techniques. Yet the counselor may believe that the client, when all is said and done, will be better off for having been fooled and so makes a decision to act without the client's permission.

Erickson (1980) noted that many powerful techniques eventually boomeranged if done primarily for his own benefit rather than for the client's. He found that people resented manipulation if they had been conned into doing something that did not benefit them. But they were not resentful if they were tricked into behavior that helped them in the long run. Counselors must choose for themselves whether these paradoxical techniques are justified, basing their decisions on accurate knowlodgo of probable benefits to the client as well as consideration of the counselor's motives for wanting the client to change.

Even further toward the end of the continuum of reasonableness are techniques that create pain or anxiety. Samenow (1984) and Korn and McCorkle (1959) made it clear that criminals must feel pain, uncertainty, anxiety, and even self-disgust to undergo change. Almost any powerful technique can create pain, but the length of that pain and the benefit it carries are the key considerations in whether to induce it. Short-term pain may be necessary for long-term gain.

Though the ethical permissability of different interventions may be on a continuum, there is no guarantee that the most effective procedure will always be the most ethical. In fact, the more powerful the technique, the more potential for harm to the client and, therefore, the more likely the technique could be used unethically.

It is our belief that reasonable efforts to "persuade" an involuntary client to participate in counseling are, in fact, humanitarian and ethical. It is not unethical to try to help someone see what is in his or her best interest through reasoning or rapport-building. The assumption that clients must be motivated to participate before counseling can begin is simplistic and ignores the reality of the presence of thousands of coerced clients in numerous settings. It remains to be seen whether there are techniques to help involuntary clients become more voluntary.

4

Defining Resistance

Chapter Four

A useful place to begin the study of the reluctant client is with an examination of the sources of resistance to change. It may seem obvious that a client forced into counseling would be resistant. But the term resistance has multiple meanings that need clarification before focusing on what to do about it.

INVOLUNTARINESS AND RESISTANCE

As discussed earlier, psychological literature exists on the problem of resistance, but there is very little on the subject of involuntariness and the resistance this brings. As Brehm (1966) noted, this lack of attention is surprising because of the value our society places on freedom. On the other hand, it is perhaps not too surprising when we consider how little credence psychological theory gives to free will and choice, which have been largely ignored in scientific efforts to find predictable, measurable causes of human behavior. Yet if asked, most people would assert that they have at least some control over their behavior, though hard pressed to say how this volition works and what its limits are.

But as Brehm noted, when people "perceive" restrictions or loss of freedom, they react, and this reaction may lead to resistance.

The importance of perceived loss of freedom can be seen by examining the effect that important life transitions have on people. At every major juncture in life, choices must be made that eventually restrict other choices. For example, when one buys a house, there is a certain loss of mobility and discretionary money. People frequently comment that such a purchase causes them to be "strapped for cash," indicating the perceived restriction of the situation. Certainly there are benefits to owning the home, but there are disadvantages also. The same is true for getting married, often referred to as "tying the knot," and for having children, who "tie us down." There is always ambivalence about making a decision that has important benefits but also significant restrictions.

Some interpersonal interactions also have the effect of limiting perceived freedom. Most of us dislike being told that we shouldn't feel angry or resentful or however we feel because we view our feelings as our own and don't want others trying to control us. Double binds have insidious effects because the restriction of our mental freedom is below awareness but not less irritating. The joke about the mother who gives her son two neckties for Christmas illustrates the problem. When he wears one tie, she remarks, "Didn't you like the other tie?" He is in a no-win situation and lacks the freedom to make a choice without having to explain himself. Still other examples of the restriction of freedom are the overprotective parent who won't allow a child to make a mistake and the parent who plans his or her children's lives by channeling them into sports and even careers without regard for their natural interests. Thus, for the involuntary client, counseling is perceived as a significant loss of freedom and this creates resentment and often rebellion, sometimes below the client's awareness. But resistance may have functional or survival value, too.

The necessity of resistance

Resistance to change is necessary; otherwise, people would change willy-nilly, and society could not tolerate the resulting upheaval and unpredictability. A person's resistance to change represents at least a degree of stability and integration of personality (Ansbacher, 1982). Resistance has positive value and a counselor should expect to find some good reasons why clients don't change—at least from their point of view.

Indeed, for many clients, counseling is threatening precisely because it is equated with confrontation of change. Delinquent teenagers may reject counseling because they have learned in their families that discussion of feelings and problems leads invariably to conflict. In their view, it is better not to talk at all than to end up fighting. Such a position may have real survival value for someone from a family intolerant of differences in viewpoints.

Resistance can also seem more understandable when we stop to appreciate how hard human beings must work to construct coherent, cohesive explanations for events in a very confusing world. Humans have always invented theories to try to understand their world. Religions in their various forms have served to help us feel as though we understand the meaning of personal as well as impersonal events. And despite the failure of science to prove it can solve the world's major social problems, many people persist in believing it can. But whether our faith is in a religion or science or a combination of the two, we are slow to change views in which we have invested much energy.

Of course, each person has a unique view of the world, but there are general patterns and styles of dealing with the uncertainty about the purpose of our existence. Generally speaking, people will develop their belief systems in one of three ways: (1) Accept an explanation for the way the world operates, perhaps a religion, invented by someone else; (2) Live without explanations and codes of behavior in an ambiguous world; or (3) Invent an explanation of their own or modify someone else's.

People who have somehow constructed a theory to explain their world will resist changing that theory because it works for them at least some of the time, and because they have already invested themselves in it, even if current circumstances persuasively argue against the validity of their world view. No one wants to start a project over if it can be salvaged and made workable. For example, if we believe that all Communist countries are dangerous and menacing, we may interpret any conciliatory statement from one of them as designed to throw us off guard. This notion is easier to incorporate into our belief system than to believe we were wrong entirely.

Resistance to change, then, is normal, necessary, and expected in human society.

AN OVERVIEW OF RESISTANCE IN CLINICAL WORK

The term resistant seems to have become a clinical catch-all to describe any client behavior or verbalization contrary to the wishes or aims of the counselor (Anderson and Stewart, 1983). Whether any counselor can or should in practice provide a totally accepting and nonjudgmental position is debatable. But from a logical point of view, it is clear that counselors who identify a client as "resistant" implicitly acknowledge their wish for the client to change. From a practical viewpoint, referral of an individual into the activity of counseling implies a need for change, though the referral source, the counselor, and the client may have different views about what changes specifically are needed. As long as there are differences in views or perceived differences in views between the counselor and client, there is fertile ground for resistance.

According to Dyer and Vriend (1973), most counselors agree that establishment of an appropriate voluntary relationship is crucial to the success of counseling. The problem with this assumption is that many clients are reluctant to begin with. Reluctance is defined as involuntariness or the prospective client not wanting to be a client in the first place. The most obvious forms of resistance are open hostility, silence, strained civility, defensiveness, avoidance, and silliness. Why is such inappropriate behavior displayed?

1. Clients must make some decisions about themselves in therapy, thereby causing them to admit to some weakness they have.
2. If referred to counseling by a third party, they may become reluctant in order to prove that party wrong.
3. The client may be fighting the "system" and view the counselor as a representative of the system.
4. If he or she resists, the client may be supported by another source.

Dyer and Vriend continued by saying that the counselor is most likely to fail when he or she takes the reluctance personally. A lack of time may make a counselor impatient with the client. Then it becomes much easier to ignore the problem rather than deal with it. But probably the biggest reason given for failure is lack of training to deal with reluctance. To succeed, the counselor must be aware of negative feelings. He or she must then develop ways of identifying when a client is being reluctant, and develop techniques to assist focusing on the problem and dealing with it.

Clients may also avoid counseling or resist changing in counseling because of their difficulties with intimacy. For many people it feels safer to reject someone trying to help them than to risk accepting that help only to be disappointed. Such clients try to create physical and emotional distance in relationships. Paradoxically, a warm and empathic counselor often is met with barriers to bonding in the therapeutic relationship, and too much pursuit of the client to bring about intimacy only intensifies the client's anxiety.

Vanier (1985), speaking of this problem with handicapped people, commented:

> It is impossible to break down the inner barricade of another. Certainly, the love, goodness, and firmness of adults who confirm and give security are indispensable, but the free compliance of the person, even if that person is severely handicapped, is also necessary. Here we touch the secret place of each one's personal freedom. Some

people are attached to their blockages and their prisons; they prefer the familiar to the unknown. It seems easier to remain in the slavery of sadness than dare to advance in insecurity along the road to liberation. Some pleasures, like drugs, briefly give a feeling of life, of well-being. It is difficult to free oneself from these seductive pleasures which lead not to life, but to death.

Resistance predicted by the way people learn

Operant learning theory provides another avenue for understanding why human behavior is often resistant to change. Though a behavior may produce many negative consequences, it may also produce some strong positive effects. A child may throw temper tantrums, for example, and dislike the spanking provoked by them, but enjoy the attention that mother and father give while administering the punishment, thus making the tantrums resistant to change. Disabled people may sometimes resist rehabilitation because it would require a return to work and a loss of disability compensation. This "secondary gain" is a factor to be studied when a behavior seems deeply entrenched. It is always important to speculate about what clients get for acting as they do, and wonder what the payoffs are, both positive and negative. These reinforcements may not be apparent at first glance, but will eventually reveal themselves if the counselor is reflective and patient.

Another reason people are often resistant to change can be understood by examining differences in the power of long-term versus short-term consequences. People are able to make the connection between an action and a consequence if the consequence follows quickly. But if the consequence comes days, months, or even years later, learning is not as efficient. For example, if we eat a food that makes us sick shortly after its consumption, we quickly learn to avoid that food. But foods that are high in cholesterol or dangerous additives sicken us slowly. Consequently, it is hard to get people to avoid foods or drugs whose effects are long delayed. Similarly, the negative consequences of many social behaviors are not immediately felt. A man may erupt in anger and achieve his immediate goal of getting his spouse to be quiet or his children to stop asking for treats. In the long run, however, this intimidation erodes relationships. But the immediate reinforcement that follows the display of anger is stronger than the negative consequences that follow sometime later. Change is resisted because destructive behaviors often have immediate positive payoff.

Many people seem controlled by the positive reinforcement of behaviors that are destructive in the long run. And many people are unable to make a meaningful cognitive link between behaviors and delayed reinforcement, thus they are unable to work for delayed gratification and will seem resistant to efforts to coax them into such behaviors as displaying patience, saving money, etc. But Vanier (1985) pointed to a more subtle problem: the inability of people to forego superficial pleasure for deeper satisfactions. Western society seems focused on material pleasures at the expense of the deeper pleasures that come from personal relationships and service to others. Getting clients to give up superficial pleasures that block movement to seeking deeper satisfactions is a difficult task and one that clients resist because they cannot see what they are missing.

Behaviorists frequently hold that attitudes and beliefs do not need to be changed in order to effect behavioral change. Thus, if a client is ordered into treatment for sex offenses, aversive stimuli can be applied when the subject becomes inappropriately aroused. Physiological arousal is measured by penile erection, galvanic skin response or other such tests, therefore no voluntary cooperation is needed to change behavior because the properly applied aversive stimulus conditions the arousal directly (Kramer, 1985). The subject soon learns not to get excited at improper objects, otherwise electric shock or noxious smells follow.

Without getting into moral or theoretical critiques of these methods, it is apparent that such methods are not in fact used on totally involuntary clients. Kramer acknowledged that subjects for his successful sex offender study were self-screened; that is, they were willing to undergo treatment if for no other reason than that the creature comforts of the treatment facility were nicer than those of the prison. The client may show some cooperation in order to get such benefits of the treatment program. If change can be brought about anyway under these conditions, then "voluntariness" becomes merely a matter of the client submitting thoughtlessly and passively to behavioral conditioning. But most counselors believe that cognitive and attitudinal change is related to behavioral change, and that some degree of active participation is necessary before comprehensive change can occur. This is recognized increasingly by even hard-core behaviorists (Wachtel, 1984). Moreover, people who are truly unwilling to submit to such aversive conditioning could probably find legal mechanisms to avoid being forced into it. The bottom line is that a minimal degree of voluntariness must be achieved before treatment can proceed in most cases.

Is the resistance conscious or willful?

In intrapsychic counseling approaches, resistance to change is viewed as residing inside the client. That is, there is thought to be some psychological mechanism or process that results in the client being uncooperative. According to psychodynamic theory, the resistance is unconscious, beyond the client's awareness. In other words, the client's intransigence is not willful. Generally speaking, the client's defense mechanisms (denial, intellectualization, reaction formation) prevent awareness of unacceptable thoughts and impulses that would be painful to experience consciously. In psychodynamic therapy, the client's relationship with the counselor (analyst) will reflect the nature of the client's internal processes. This process is called transference (Strean, 1985). Resistance is an expected result of the client's style of projecting his internal processes onto the counselor (analyst). Clients may rebel against their counselors as they have toward parental authority figures, even though the counselor's behavior in reality has been neutral and nonauthoritarian.

Other causes of resistance in psychodynamic theory are the result of the id, ego, and superego. The id creates resistance because of its infantile desire for gratification that resists delayed gratification. The ego protects the person from the breakthrough into behavior of unacceptable sexual and aggressive impulses, but of course, these impulses stubbornly find expression elsewhere. The superego creates self-critical punishment-seeking that resists rational efforts to control it (Strean, 1985).

This psychodynamic model, however, does not seem to fit as well for involuntary clients whose uncooperativeness often appears quite conscious and willful. For example, many people on probation are required to submit to urine tests to check for drug use. A client who misses a counseling appointment, then claims to have "forgotten," may in fact have missed the meeting and lied about the reason. Having recently taken drugs, a client would be foolish to submit to incriminating tests. Of course, it could be argued that although the lying was consciously done, the true motivation for the need to defy authority is yet unconscious. Nevertheless, the resistance to the counselor (probation officer) is not explained convincingly in all cases by a psychodynamic model. However, Larke (1985) gave a persuasive review of literature on treating the mandated client from a psychodynamic perspective, emphasizing borderline and narcissistic disorders.

Cognitive counseling theories also hold that resistance is intrapsychic. Ellis' rational-emotive therapy (1985), for example, clearly recognizes the concept of resistance, and in fact, expects resistance because of the client's irrational beliefs, e.g., that the world should be fair or that one shouldn't make mistakes. It does seem sensible to expect people with strong irrational beliefs to resist change because change would require a restructuring of their view of the world. This restructuring requires energy. Ellis' approach is for the therapist to meet the client's resistance with enough energy to overcome the barriers to change. The therapist attempts to vigorously persuade the client to change beliefs by logical challenges of those beliefs.

Ellis identified several irrational beliefs that contribute to resistance to counseling. Some of these beliefs are: "It shouldn't be so hard to change;" "I must change quickly, and if I don't I'm worthless;" or "No one should force me to do what I don't want to, and it's horrible if they do." Ellis commented that the major resistances could be traced to low frustration tolerance, stemming from the belief that things should be easy and quick (I want what I want when I want it), and from distress about being distressed, stemming from the belief that one should be perfect. Ellis' approach is to challenge these false beliefs through rational-emotive therapy, which essentially calls for the counselor and client to dispute the false beliefs and create new, more sensible ones in order to attain an emotionally healthy belief system. Usually in rational-emotive therapy, it is considered important that the client understand the theoretical connection between irrational beliefs and unhealthy emotions, so that the correction of irrational beliefs can generalize to other areas in the person's life through application of the method. With the involuntary client, however, it may be necessary to teach the system later and challenge specific beliefs as needed to get the counseling started.

However, Patterson (1980) raised two important questions about this approach. First, he argued that long-lasting change occurs when clients draw their own conclusions rather than have someone else do it for them, as seems to happen in the direct teaching style of rational-emotive therapy. Second, much research points to the importance of the client/counselor relationship as a central ingredient bringing about change in counseling, and Patterson noted his own belief that Ellis' results were more influenced by the therapeutic relationship than Ellis is willing to admit. Also, though Ellis' approach is effective with many clients, he acknowledged less effectiveness with unmotivated, antisocial personalities who are experiencing no psychic discomfort as a result of their irrational beliefs.

Resistance sometimes seems to be the result of the behavior of people in a particular role. Take, for example, the classic case of probationers who are told by supervising probation officers to trust them. Trust, of course, cannot be summoned in the same way an employer demands and secures punctuality from employees. The result of the order is to increase the client's resentment and suspicion. The roles in which the officer and probationer find themselves are inherently adversarial because of the power the officer holds over the probationer. It is no surprise that the probationer resists the directive to trust the supervising officer. Probationers will likely be quite conscious of their apprehensions, but find themselves unable to think of any way to change their situation because their status as a probationer is beyond their control. Likewise, probation officers find themselves in the awkward position of being both counselor and policeman, and there is little they can do about this either except to acknowledge the conflict and proceed. In some cases, then, resistance may be more conveniently explained by conflict of social roles and social interactions rather than by internal psychological processes.

Resistance as a function of the aim of counseling

Another way of thinking about resistance concerns the kind of change intended by the counseling process. Some counseling approaches seek to change patterns of behavior or reconstruct personality. On the other end of the continuum are counseling approaches that attempt to engage the client in a problem-solving discussion. (Sometimes the former approach is called psychotherapy while the latter is called counseling. This dichotomy is useful conceptually but in clinical practice it is difficult to tell the difference.) When counselors attempt to reconstruct personality, as in psychodynamic approaches, resistance is the personality's defense against awareness of unacceptable thoughts or desires. Resistance in the reconstruction model is likely to be observed more as counseling progresses, as the personality unfolds.

In the problem-solving model, the resistance may either be nonexistent, or for involuntary clients, concentrated in the early stages of the change process as counselor and client clarify their respective expectations and needs. If clients learn that there will be no attempt to affect their personalities and if the counselor presents no material threat, like revocation of probation, then there is no reason not to talk about the problems that were the reason for referral into counseling. This is so even if clients do not yet acknowledge their responsibility for their problems. If, as the counseling progresses, it begins to cause shifts in perceptions, then clients will resist new perceptions that demand formation of a new identity or change of crucial, centrally-held beliefs and values. Then the nature of the resistance changes, becoming more of a resistance to change than a resistance to counseling in the abstract.

Pekarik (1985) discussed the importance of client and counselor sharing similar expectations in regard to therapeutic objectives and expected length of treatment. Clients prefer short-term, crisis resolution counseling, while counselors prefer longer treatment that focuses on changing basic personality or behavioral patterns. As a result, many clients drop out of treatment dissatisfied and are considered "resistant."

This discussion about the kind of change intended by counseling is presented merely as a useful way to think about the nature of resistance. Strict advocates of a particular theory might argue that the client's personality creates resistance from the very first session. But this is a limited point of view that tends to obscure simpler explanations for behavior. Counselors need to examine practices that clients routinely rebel against, especially in the early stages of treatment. Put simply, any counseling practice that is threatening, degrading, dehumanizing, demeaning, impolite, or generally annoying will elicit resistance. Antagonistic receptionists, excessive paperwork, and long waits for appointments are just a few examples of practices that cause problems. Before attempting complicated maneuvers to manage resistance, it is important to look for straightforward, simple solutions based on principles of respect and courtesy.

It should be noted again that reluctance to enter counseling does not necessarily mean the same as resistance in counseling. Many clients who do not choose to enter counseling quickly become eager to solve problems and to work once in counseling. Many voluntary clients, on the other hand, are quite resistant to change, though the resistance is generally covert. Sometimes, though the resistance is rather indirect, it is very obvious. A colleague tells the story of a client who explained that he had not read a recommended article because he was afraid it would change his mind! This "Don't confuse me with facts, my mind is made up" reaction is not uncommon. It is too simple to say that the involuntary client is always more resistant than the voluntary client. Sometimes those who say they want to change really do not, and those who say they do not want to change really do. But in general, the involuntary client would be expected to show some special resistance to the idea of counseling, even though all clients will resist change.

Haley (1963) raised the question of whether anyone wholeheartedly volunteers for counseling since most people enter counseling because of pressure generated by a problem or person. A synopsis of Haley's discussion summarizes his views on paradoxes inherent to psychotherapy and the issue of voluntariness. Haley said that when a patient attends psychotherapy, it is usually under duress. This makes the relationship compulsory, yet the relationship is described as voluntary. This paradox is shown by the following situations:

1. The client is told that the relationship is voluntary. He/she is told that he/she doesn't have to come to the session if he/she doesn't want to. Yet

when he/she misses a session, pressure is put on him/her to attend the "voluntary" session.

2. The client wonders if the therapist is seeing him/her by choice or because he/she gets paid for it. The therapist gives the patient the impression that it is by choice. Yet the therapist has no interest in the client outside the office.

3. The relationship of client and counselor is neither inflicting blame nor removing it. Yet both implications are present simultaneously. The patients are treated as if they cannot help behaving as they do. At the same time, the therapy is based on the premise that patients can help what they do; that is why they are receiving treatment.

4. In therapy, the client meets an expert who, paradoxically, takes charge of the session by placing the patient in charge.

5. The therapy itself is like no other life experience, yet the therapist wonders why the patient doesn't respond in ordinary ways.

6. In therapy, a patient is supposed to relate all of his/her weaknesses to someone who apparently doesn't have any.

Resistance and limitation of choice

There is another rule of thumb about resistance that seems to transcend issues such as whether counseling is reconstructive or problem-oriented and whether resistance is situational or internal: the limitation of choice. When clients perceive consciously or unconsciously that their freedom to choose is being restricted, they resist (Brehm, 1966). The goal of counseling, if not to expand the client's perceptions of options, should at least be not to restrict them or to provoke the client's reluctance to being controlled. Otherwise, change to more acceptable behavior will be hindered as clients struggle to regain control and autonomy. For example, family counselors may elicit resistance merely by requiring that all family members attend all sessions because it is likely that at least some family members would rather be someplace else. Even highly irresponsible clients must see that responsible living is a choice with benefits, otherwise counseling will fail.

If a primary source of resistance to counseling is the client's perception of being forced to do something against his or her will, then the way to avoid resistance is to alter clients' perceptions in such a way that they begin to want to do whatever they weren't doing before counseling or stop whatever they were doing. The difficulty in counseling is not in knowing what needs to be changed but in knowing how to stimulate cooperation in working toward change. But how does the counselor get the client to agree to cooperate and then to begin to change? As long as clients feel coerced, they will resist cooperating. Geiser (1985) noted that mandated treatment was necessary to create a period of sustained involvement in which responsibility issues could be addressed. But forcing participation is just the first step to gaining cooperation and change.

Resistance as a function of the amount of change needed

It was stated earlier that people fall into three groups: those who blindly accept external belief systems, those who have no coherent belief systems, and those who have developed their own belief systems. Since all counseling requires or implies a change in belief systems, it becomes important to anticipate how much change is needed because extensive change requires the expenditure of great energy and hence provokes high resistance.

This grouping of people into three categories is, of course, simplistic, but other points of view lead to essentially the same conclusion. Menninger (1968) pointed out that criminal behavior is motivated in large part by an enormous feeling of helplessness that offenders are unable to manage because of undeveloped adaptation skills. Consequently, they are often unable to improve their situation without violence, and they respond aggressively to any restriction that seems to control or dominate them. Thus, the lack of development and integration of personality signals the need for much change. But the very mention of that need to the offender implies control and restriction against which the offender chafes and rebels because he sees the problem as external to himself.

Offenders usually feel wronged by the society that forced them into treatment, and they also consciously fear any incriminating disclosure that could be used against them. These clients, who must substantially alter beliefs about society, family, or past life events, will present more resistance than clients under temporary stress needing situational adjustment. The client who views the police as agents of a repressive society needs to change substantially to relate effectively with others, and in fact will vigorously resist change because the problem is viewed as external to self and therefore outside self-control. In short, the more the client views the problem as external to self, the greater the need for change.

So far, then, several tools for thinking about resistance have been reviewed: (1) Is the resistance inside the client and encountered as counseling attempts to reconstruct personality or world view? Or is the resistance more appropriately understood by looking at the roles played by counselor and client? (2) Is the resistance unconscious or is the client aware of it? Is the resistance willful? (3) In what way does counseling provoke resistance by affecting clients' perceptions of their ability to choose and threatening their sense of dignity and autonomy? (4) How much change is needed in the client? How much effort will that change require of the client? To what extent does the client view the problem as externally caused?

These are issues that arise from examination of individually oriented therapies. However, family systems theory opens up a new vista for understanding resistance to treatment and thus another tool for thinking about resistance: How does the family system resist change?

Family systems and resistance

Sometimes it seems as though factors outside people play a part in their resistance to counseling and change. The juvenile delinquent who resists expressions of feeling in order to avoid conflict may be following a family rule that is still given support by other family members. Consequently, the counselor will not comprehend the delinquent's reluctance to participate in counseling without first understanding the conspiracy of the entire family to ensure silence. What function does the silence have for the entire family? Who is protected by the silence?

These questions are not easily answered, or even asked, by traditional, individually oriented, intraspsychic counseling approaches that focus on the client's individual feelings, beliefs, and behaviors. The family systems approach, however, attempts to understand behavior in the context of significant others. Family therapists believe that trying to understand people without examining their family is like trying to understand one character in a play without the dialogue of other characters.

Anderson and Stewart (1983) wrote a comprehensive examination of resistance from the family therapy perspective. They stated that family therapists make two basic assumptions about families: first, people are influenced by the history of their family of origin and by the history of their own marital relationship; second, families organize themselves both to reinforce the individual identities of their members and to ensure the survival of the family as a unit. Though there is no clear consensus on the definition of resistance in the various schools of family therapy (as there is none in the individual, intrapsychic therapies), Anderson and Stewart's synthesis of common threads in family therapy has value because it identifies two themes that relate to resistance: habit and homeostasis.

The historical view of families shows ingrained, habitual, and largely unconscious patterns of relating that provide families with a sense of security and predictability. Habits that are many years old, sometimes many generations old, will resist change. Much of a family's ideology or belief system survives from past generations. The family is the vehicle of cultural transmission, passing on beliefs about work, religion, children, and so on. Families that are traditionally Catholic, for example, tend to stay that way, just as certain states are traditionally Democratic or Republican. William James noted that habit is the great flywheel of society, implying that habit is important for understanding momentum in the social order.

Understanding the structure of families also assists understanding of the homeostatic processes that regulate family processes. Homeostasis is a process of self-regulation by which the family maintains stability by giving corrective feedback to family members. For example, parents sometimes resist letting their children change and grow up by giving them messages to stay as they are. Viewed at a particular point in time, the hierarchical structure of a family tends to organize itself in a particular pattern and attempts to stay that way. Thus, the roles of mothers and fathers as parents are distinguished from the roles of children and grandparents.

The tasks of family members are dictated by the family structure, providing definition and therefore a tacit understanding of expectations. The eldest female child is seldom directly told she must watch out for her younger siblings, but she learns these caretaking behaviors as a result of her position in the family structure. If she attempts to change and unilaterally redefine her responsibilities in the family, the other members will attempt to get her to resume her expected role. The family's rules do not change easily.

These family rules can be discovered by examining interactions and sequences of behaviors among the members. Each time a teenager runs away from home, it is observed that a conflictual relationship between mother and father improves as they cooperate to bring the errant youngster home. After a period of relative calm, the parents will reignite their conflict and the teenager repeats the behavior designed to bring them together. In treatment, family members will avoid the counselor's efforts to focus on the key problems and may terminate counseling if pressured to talk about them.

Elkin (1984) characterized the alcoholic family system as a conspiracy of silence in which the alcoholic member exercises power through drunkenness because there is no easy method for family members to confront and deal with the behavior of the alcoholic. But the power of the alcoholic generally goes unnoticed until the effects on the family are observed in reaction to the drinking. It is important to recognize the value of a family systems point of view in understanding why people may be reluctant to discuss issues deemed critical by the counselor. Many of the ideas discussed later derive from innovations in family therapy.

In general, resistance of a client in counseling may be conceptualized from a systems point of view as occurring whenever change threatens to break the client's unspoken family rules or change the family's structure, which are pressured to remain the same.

Our attention now turns back to some basic but often forgotten concepts about communication.

5

Inhibitors and Facilitators of Communication

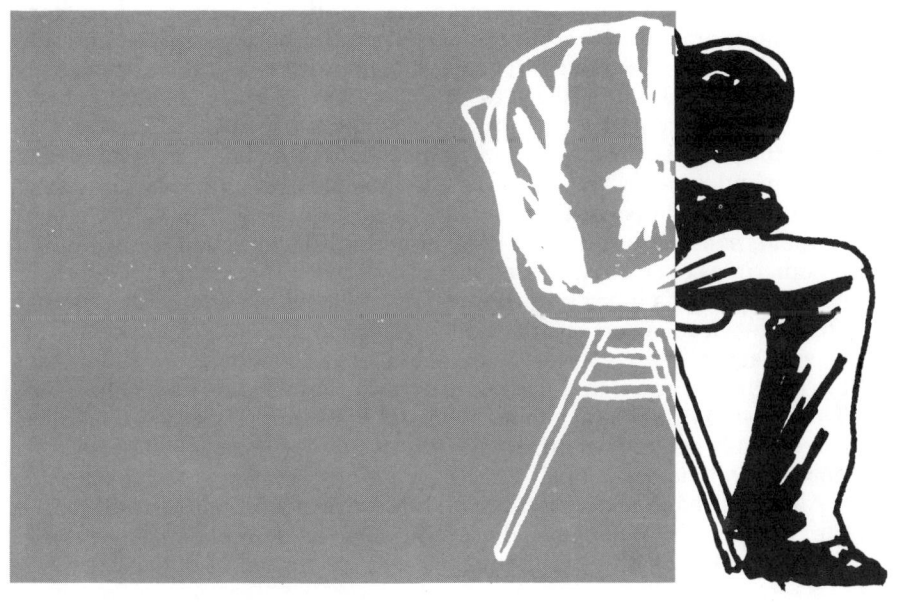

Chapter Five

Since counseling requires communication, it will be helpful to look at factors that generally inhibit and facilitate communication, particularly in an interview. Gorden (1980) defined a number of inhibitors and facilitators, and a review of these will provide a useful backdrop and help generate practical suggestions for counselors.

THE INHIBITORS

Competing demands for time

No interview will be successful when the participants have other, more important (at least to them) demands on their attention. This is true for both client and counselor. The number of things that compete for attention are enormous: ringing telephones, a waiting friend, a hungry stomach, an interesting television show. Counselors should be sure they have no interruptions, such as phone calls, to detract from the interviews. Counselors need to be able to concentrate on the work at hand.

But counselors should also be sensitive to their clients' needs. A teenager who has to miss a big basketball game or pep rally to attend counseling will probably be thinking more about the score than about counseling. Though it is not possible to schedule appointments to avoid interference with every commitment or interest the client may have, it is important to avoid major competing demands on time and attention. Whenever some external factor seems to be interfering with the effectiveness of the session, it is important to deal with it, if at all possible.

Etiquette

Earlier, the need for counselors to avoid demeaning, derogatory statements or actions was mentioned. Though this need for tact and sensitivity seems self-evident, it is surprising how often counselors ignore the impact of labels and negative descriptions on their clients. In one psychological report, the examiner expressed dismay that the client abruptly left the interview room, slamming the door behind her. The psychologist said he had "merely been reporting the results of testing which revealed an underlying sense of fragility and incompetence."

Clients sense disapproval or condemnation, and although confrontation is sometimes necessary, it does less good if it diminishes the client's self-esteem and adds a brick in the wall of resistance. It is no surprise that clients feel fragile and unsure of themselves, and it should also be no surprise that they react angrily when told things so rudely. Manners and tact are important, and if they are not exhibited, there should be good reason. Though some antisocial people do mistake kindness for weakness, this is no reason to imitate the criminal's tactics in interpersonal relations. It is possible to hold one's position firmly but not cruelly.

All people have customs that structure ways of doing things and define the type of topics that can be discussed. Most of us would stiffen if a total stranger asked us how much money we make. So, too, clients in counseling will be resistant to untimely and insensitive forays into forbidden territory. Counselors sometimes forget how intrusive their questions are, perhaps because counseling becomes routine and, after a while, the sensitivity of certain topics is forgotten. Counselors who do a great deal of sexual counseling forget that the average person is not accustomed to hearing such words as orgasm, vagina, or penis in public. Many people also are raised with the belief that "dirty linen shouldn't be aired in public" and this belief does inhibit willingness to discuss personal problems, especially in group counseling. Some clients will hide themselves by claiming that they do not discuss personal matters with strangers and counselors must learn to differentiate between truly embarrassed clients and those who feign it.

Used properly, attention to etiquette can become a facilitator of communication. People will respond to sharing of food or drink, for example, as an age-old custom that creates bonds of friendship. Politeness communicates respect and fosters trust. Counselors who smoke should not impose their smoking on their clients without permission, and asking permission establishes a measure of reciprocity and equality, at least on matters of custom.

Trauma

Sometimes an upsetting episode seems to close the valve that regulates the vocal cords. People cannot stop talking about their near-miss in a car wreck or fall down the stairs. But the trauma of arrest, trial, and conviction is painful to remember and is therefore suppressed. Clients may not want to talk about traumatic experiences that are embarrassing or that, if thought about, will require action in the present. Rape victims will often resist "working through" their experience because of the unpleasantness of the anger that is aroused, not to mention the memory of the pain, fear, and humiliation. Many people believe that trying to forget unpleasant events is the best policy, a belief that naively ignores that trust must be rebuilt and that emotional pain cannot be covered up or swept away.

Counselors need to respect the protective quality of resistance to talk after some traumas while remembering that sometimes clients need to be prodded to review and discuss painful material. Of course, a client may sometimes consciously and willfully avoid talking about certain subjects on the pretext that to do so would be painful. Offenders may try to avoid talking about their criminal record, not because they would feel pain in doing so, but because they do not want to.

Cultural differences

Significant cultural or social differences between client and counselor may inhibit communication severely enough to make the counselor think the client is resistant. American Indians from certain tribes, such as the Apache, tend not to be highly self-disclosing to non-Indians. Clients from low social and economic groups may be mistrustful or resentful of counselors who appear to have had all the advantages of middle-class life, and certainly many counselors raised in the middle class may not understand the special problems of those raised in poverty. Whites may not understand blacks (or vice versa); men may be insensitive to women's issues (or vice versa). All these factors are important considerations in counseling the involuntary client, whose resistance is made worse by misunderstanding or by anticipated misunderstanding. An excellent article by Vontress (1974) gives additional details on cultural and social differences.

THE FACILITATORS

Fulfilling expectations

A person holding darts and standing in the middle of a square room is more likely to hit the target if he or she knows which wall the target is on. Likewise, clients are more likely to be cooperative if they have an idea of what direction to proceed, assuming there are no negative influences blocking movement in that direction. Yet many poorly educated and psychologically unsophisticated clients do not have a clear idea about what is done in counseling and may expect the counselor to give advice like a physician gives a prescription.

As Pekarik (1985) indicated, discrepant expectations between counselor and client about duration and goals of treatment are a factor causing premature termination. Addressing those discrepancies or adjusting treatment to the client's expectations (such as providing brief therapy) may increase effectiveness. A certain amount of structure is necessary for the conduct of counseling: appointment times, fees, cancellation policies, length of sessions, number of anticipated sessions, confidentiality issues, etc. Counselors will vary on whether to suggest topics for discussion or define the problems, but at a minimum counselors should try to understand the expectations the client brings to counseling, including expectations that may be inconsistent with those of the counselor.

Many expectations are communicated indirectly. Counselors can communicate their expectation that counseling will be successful or unsuccessful, fun or painful through the tone they use as much as their specific words. Consequently, it is important for counselors to examine their own attitudes by noting their prognosis for a case. Though the success rate for certain clients may not be good statistically, it is important to approach each client as a potential success. Otherwise, one will never know whether the counseling was influenced by prejudgment.

Sympathetic understanding

Most people respond positively to being and feeling understood. Empathy has been widely studied as a key factor in successful counseling. However, difficult clients are sometimes not very appealing, and counselors therefore have trouble feeling empathic. Belligerent teenagers can be extremely frustrating clients and people who have committed serious criminal offenses can be morally repugnant. The involuntary client often enters counseling unable to show the softer, likable features that would bring out the counselor's understanding. Duehn and Proctor (1977) found that nonempathic counselors have a high rate of early termination from counseling. Epperson et al. (1983) emphasized the importance of counselors to be able to accurately rate the client's perceptions of his problems—an important indicator of accurate empathy. Perhaps no other single factor is as important as empathy in working with the involuntary, resistant client.

New experience

Many people respond positively to the opportunity to do new things. Though involuntary clients may on the surface regard counseling with dread, there may be an underlying curiosity about themselves that can be capitalized on. Many of the popular techniques of the therapeutic professions may help pique curiosity: hypnosis, biofeedback, psychological testing, empty chair techniques, psychodrama, structured exercise and feedback, and dream work, to name just a few. Counselors can clip and use questionnaires from newspapers and popular magazines, not because they reliably measure attitudes, beliefs, or psychological conditions, but because they do arouse curiosity and stimulate discussion.

Use of gimmicks should never get in the way of counseling, but a certain amount of showmanship may be constructive. More important, many clients, once into the process, discover that talking about personal matters to a trustworthy and intelligent listener is a worthwhile new experience in its own right (Menninger, 1958). With young clients, the counselor should remember that they were raised in an era of visual stimulation. Videotaping of sessions introduces a novelty that will appeal to some. Movies or videotapes of speakers or dramatic presentations may expose some clients to ideas where assigned reading would fail. Use of other visual aids in counseling, such as flip charts, also provides a break from the routine of talking.

Need for meaning

Anthropologists have long noted that human societies construct explanations for natural phenomena through religion, science, or other belief systems. This need is probably not equally strong in all individuals, however. As noted before, some people simply accept the beliefs taught by religion, government, or parents. Other people struggle to develop their own viewpoints, with varying degrees of success. Still others seem to operate without principles, values, or guiding beliefs.

Many clients who are involuntary referrals are really struggling very hard to develop a way of living, but unsuccessfully. The counselor can appeal to these clients by encouraging them to talk about their confusion with their beliefs. This request appeals to their need to understand the meaning of events in their lives. This technique is probably the core of most existential therapy. However, poorly educated clients who also have a low level of abstract thinking ability will probably not respond as well to philosophical discussion as they will to learning though active experience. Participants in a work release program, for example, may not develop a conceptual appreciation of the value of work in helping them feel that they are contributing to society, but this feeling may emerge as paychecks are actually earned and received and payments are made to support children and meet other obligations.

The inhibitors and facilitators of communication are largely based on common sense. But as Will Rogers once said, common sense is unfortunately not common practice. It never hurts to be reminded of simple, practical strategies to help people talk.

6

Resistance in Beginning Sessions

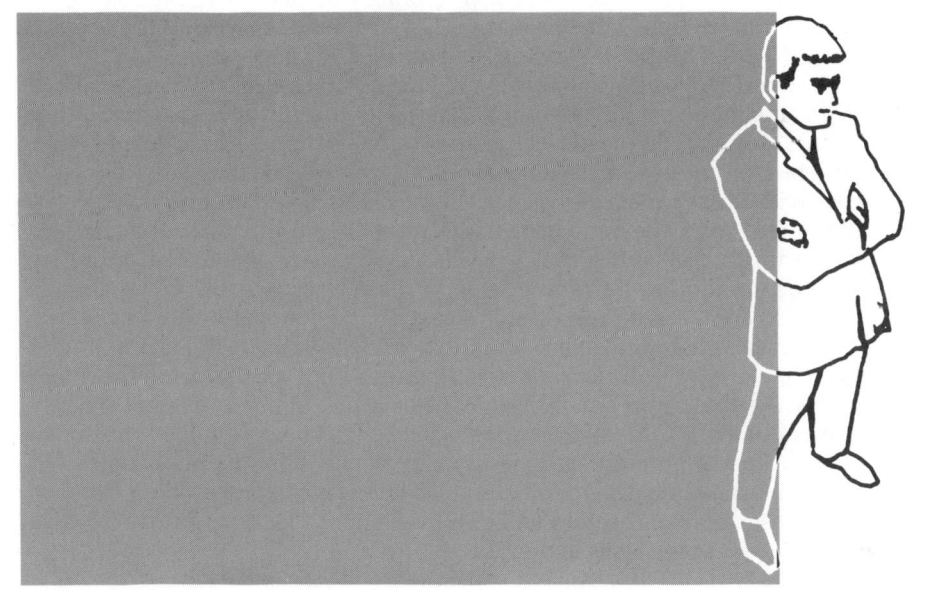

Chapter Six

With the nature of resistance defined and comments made about general factors that affect communication, attention now turns to the first counseling interviews, the point at which the counselor initially encounters resistance, especially with involuntary clients. Of course, clients are often resistant even before the first session. They may, for instance, miss appointments or rehearse their opening performances long before seeing the counselor.

Strean (1985) offered an insightful analysis of clients who show their resistance over the telephone by inquiring, then complaining about fees or by being unable to find a mutually agreeable appointment time. This resistance shows a fear of therapy and ambivalence about wanting to change, but involuntary clients frequently have no opportunity to resist being compelled into treatment. Instead, they frequently remain silent and uncommunicative.

WHEN CLIENTS WILL NOT TALK

Counselors are frustrated when their clients will not volunteer enough information to get the counseling session going. Ordinarily counselors expect clients to come to counseling with a problem to work on or with enough emotion to create feelings and reactions. However, the involuntary client frequently remains reserved and passive, sometimes refusing to speak at all in hostile defiance at having been ordered to attend. Or the involuntary client may offer only minimal responses, answering simple questions with a yes or no or providing noncommittal, vague, or evasive responses to prompts from the counselor.

On the surface at least, the client appears unmotivated or passive-aggressive. Either or both descriptions may be accurate, depending on one's point of view, but there are a few strategies that sometimes elicit enough verbal output to "prime the pump" for future work. Many clients who superficially appear to be uncooperative and angry will be discovered to be amenable to counseling if gotten past their initial resistance. Other clients may have defenses or character styles that make them deeply resistant, but the counselor should not assume intractable resistance to be the case without adequate assessment of the client's personality structure. In outpatient work the counselor usually needs to try to allow the client to warm up to the counseling process. In inpatient work with more ingrained problems the milieu may be designed to control the client's behavior and create pressure to deal with the counselor in some way.

The beginning counselor's reaction to the untalkative client will tend to go in one of two directions: rejecting the client or imploring the client to talk. Neither approach is effective. Becoming angry and rejecting only drives clients into deeper silence because they feel alienated and criticized by the very person who is supposed to be there to "help" them. On the other hand, pleading with clients to talk sets a bad precedent because it indicates that counselors will assume a client's responsibility to talk in order to see themselves as helpful.

The purpose of counseling, of course, is to help the client and not to satisfy counselors' needs to enhance their self-images. Clients will sense the counselor's motive and will feel used, though it is doubtful most clients could articulate their feelings. Furthermore, counselors who become overinvested in the client's welfare set themselves up for manipulation because the client may later use whatever leverage is available. Consequently, it is important to identify strategies that elicit the client's participation without creating defensiveness and without causing the counselor to inappropriately take on the client's responsibilities. While counselors must care about their client's welfare, they must not take on the client's responsibility for his or her own problems.

Identifying reasons for not talking

The counselor's first task is to try to understand the reasons for the client's silence. The causes could include any of the following:

1. Clients resent having been forced into counseling, so they exercise the only control they have to retain a sense of individual autonomy and dignity.
2. Clients do not understand what counseling is all about and are confused about what to say, so they say nothing rather than risk appearing stupid.
3. Clients perceive no personal responsibility for the problems the referral source says they have and therefore do not see what counseling could do to fix the problem.
4. Clients are afraid that the counselor will reveal information to third parties that would be embarrassing or damaging, personally or legally.
5. Clients fear their own dependency and avoid facing that fear by acting independent.
6. Clients control the counseling by remaining silent because they have a need to dominate or embarrass the counselor.

The counselor's task is to be supremely empathic; to understand the client's dilemma given very little information or interaction. The key to being empathic is to be able to put oneself in another's position. And it is not hard to imagine why many people would be resentful, scared, or confused after being told by the courts or other powerful people, such as a school principal or social welfare authority, to enter counseling. But how do the counselors show their clients they understand these feelings?

The typical counselor wants to get right to the issues or reasons for referral without first addressing the preliminary matter of preparing the client for counseling. Remember that addressing expectations is an important facilitator of communication. Most counselors have standard opening lines, such as "Tell me what brings you here," or "How can I help you?" The involuntary client will likely answer: "The judge said I had to come," or "I don't know. You're the counselor, you tell me." When these are the client's responses to the counselor's prompts, the counselor must plan to spend some time exploring and seeking to understand the reluctance to talk, as in the following dialogue:

Counselor: (after introductions and amenities) Well, would you tell me what brings you here?
Client: You know. The judge said I had to come here.
Counselor: What's your understanding of the reason for this?
Client: I don't know.
Counselor: Did the judge say if you came here that the sentence would be suspended?
Client: Yeah.
Counselor: So what do you think you're supposed to do here?
Client: You're the counselor. I don't know.
Counselor: Well, the idea is to talk about the problem that got you into trouble.
Client: The only problem I have is how to get through this and make the judge happy.
Counselor: It must be irritating to be forced into coming here.
Client: (pause) Yeah. It's a bum deal. What good is coming here gonna do?
Counselor: So you're mad about having to talk about something when you don't think it'll help.
Client: Well, wouldn't you be?

Here, instead of grilling the client about what the problem is, the counselor focuses on the reasons for the client's resentment at being in counseling, a subject that is more immediate in the client's thoughts. The client's final question, "Well, wouldn't you be?" indicates the counselor has made contact, though more work is needed before refocusing on the reason for the referral into counseling. The counselor may be tempted at this point to agree that it is natural to feel angry at being coerced into treatment, but this reassurance must be phrased carefully so as not to condone the resentment. Counselors must differentiate themselves from the referral source to clarify their function, but yet must not be critical of the referral source. A simple statement, such as "I didn't send you here, but while you're here why don't we see what we can accomplish?" serves as a nonthreatening invitation to talk while it disassociates the counselor from the coercion.

One of the most important roadblocks to overcome in counseling is the client's pessimism about his or her ability to change and hence to feel better. This pessimism may take the form of demeaning therapy, but may show up in other ways as well, such as mild depression. Counselors who do not bring this attitude into the open will sometimes find their clients going through the motions of the process but not fully engaged. Homework assignments will seldom be done thoroughly and concentration will be weak. It is impossible to learn any complex skill without actively participating. No one ever learned to juggle by watching passively. Clients must be mentally and emotionally active before their life problems can be addressed.

Clients who are reluctant to examining their resistance or pessimism are more difficult to treat than those who begin to relate comfortably to a counselor who has identified and empathized with their pessimism.

Clients who resist talking about their unhappiness about being in treatment may be antisocial personalities or at least oppositional in nature, that is, rebellious to almost everything and everyone. In order to effectively deal with such clients it is important to understand how deep their resistance is.

Many criminal offenders use silence as a source of power. They view the counselor as a contemptible "square john." Yochelson and Samenow (1976, 1977) described a procedure in which the counselor dispassionately confronts offenders with a description of their thoughts and lifestyles while the clients remain essentially silent. For example, the counselor might describe how offenders view themselves as unique and therefore above rules that apply to others. If counselors offer an accurate assessment, they may appear to be mind readers, and this display of power elicits their clients' fascination and deprives them of the power they believe they display by remaining silent. The technique requires an in-depth understanding of criminal thinking and assumes that criminals willfully withhold information in order to control the counseling session. Yochelson and Samenow's view is harsher in regard to offenders than many counselors are willing to accept, however, and there will continue to be debates about the underlying intent of offenders.

Some counselors deal with silence by remarking that the client must be very afraid or angry and that if they sat together in silence for awhile, then that would be fine. Counselors will have varying degrees of patience for this approach, and clients ordered into a small, fixed number of sessions can simply wait out the end of the requirement. Enright and Estep (1973) outlined a technique of metered counseling in which the client got credit on the meter only when actually participating in the session. On one occasion, one of the authors required a nontalkative boy to stand during the session if he didn't have anything to say. This requirement made it easier to talk than not talk, and soon the boy found lots of things to talk about. This kind of silent client is often found in school guidance settings, clinics, and private practice when parents want their children to have counseling but the child doesn't understand, or doesn't try to understand, why.

Consequences for failure to participate

For whatever reason, there will be clients who do not respond to reasonable efforts to get them to participate. The counselor must then decide what to do about this situation. When there is a consequence for failure to complete required counseling, such as suspension from school or a threat of imprisonment, the counselor must be prepared to let the referral source know that counseling has not taken place and then not feel responsible for the consequences. It is a good practice, however, not to threaten the client. The client usually knows the consequences, and threats are destructive to the counseling relationship. A calm statement of the facts is all that is necessary.

Clients sometimes bargain with their counselor not to report them, saying, "Who'll know the difference anyway?" Many counselors feel impelled to explain their moral decision, and though there could be some value in this, the explanation will usually only get more argument. For example, if the counselor says, "I'm going to inform your probation officer that you haven't completed counseling because I agreed to report your attendance," the client may respond, "Well, I thought your job was to help people like me stay out of trouble."

Counselors' integrity must be shown through their behavior, not their explanations of their behavior. So it is important not to be sidetracked by arguments that cannot be won. But the counselor also must not compromise on issues of ethics and integrity.

Although clients should be allowed to feel the natural consequences of their actions, the counselor should not hint at or suggest any consequence that is unlikely to be carried out or that is not within the counselor's power to bring about. In some jurisdictions, failure to complete a treatment program that is a condition of parole may or may not mean revocation of parole. Workers in halfway houses are frequently faced with clients who have court-designated, firm release dates over which workers have very little control. Whenever working with an involuntary client, the counselor must know what will happen to clients who fail. Since counseling can't really be "forced" upon someone through threats anyway, the primary power the counselor needs is the power to choose not to counsel a particular client. Paradoxically, the most "powerful" counselors are often those who know they are impotent to coerce. They can only influence, and hence they avoid wasting their energy on strategies that only provoke more resistance and concentrate instead on approaches that have a chance of success, however small.

Yochelson and Samenow (1976, 1977) recommend that counselors explain the options to offenders: change, commit suicide, or continue in behavior that will ultimately lead to prison. For many involuntary clients, the options are different or not so severe. Not all involuntary clients are criminals. But the point is well taken. It is important for counselor and client to explore the probable result of failure to actively participate in treatment. Then let the chips fall where they may.

In some work situations counselors have responsibility for enforcing institutional rules, and this reality does affect the ability to be nonjudgmental of clients. As previously discussed, the counselor often has conflicting roles and there is little that can be done about it except examine the responsibility and requirements of the job and note the ramifications. Some counselors shy away from legitimate and necessary use of authority, claiming that use of authority interferes with therapy. In all likelihood this stance in its extreme represents personal uncomfortableness with power more than a theoretical position about what makes therapy effective. There is also a difference between power and authority, which Palmer (1983) asserted is necessary in the helping relationship because the counselor must have the legitimate right to make certain decisions.

It is important for counselors to carefully examine their values and be prepared to act on their principles, which sometimes will require use of authority. It is unrealistic to expect that the counseling encounter will always occur in a context without drawbacks and inconsistencies, and the sensible choice is to forge ahead in an imperfect world by making the best of the situation. If a counselor who must also sometimes be an enforcer finds this conflict unbearable, then finding another job may be the answer.

Failing to use power is as extreme as using power arrogantly or guarding it zealously, and there are many instances in which control can be shared with the client to help the counseling process proceed.

Giving away power and other ways to break the initial impasse

In all probability, despite the reality of the counselor's relative inability to force behavioral change, most clients feel intimidated by someone they perceive as more powerful. Understanding this, counselors can make some effort to "give away" power by suggesting that they "can't pull out words like dentists extract teeth." Counselors can also agree in principle to answer any question they might ask of the client—a "what's good for the goose is good for the gander" approach. If the counseling gets rolling, the counselor should guard against confusion about who is being counseled, but a sense of reciprocity can be established to remove the weight of a perceived imbalance of power. Therapists who work by interpreting transference will, of course, object to answering questions posed by clients since to do so would contaminate the transference. (As a practical matter, it is the rare involuntary client who is in treatment long enough to benefit from such analysis, assuming that it is potentially beneficial.)

Other examples of giving away power are to allow the client to choose appointment times or days or to select from a list of topics of what to discuss on a given day.

One of the authors worked with a client who was ordered into counseling and who said that "staring" (eye contact) bothered her. So it was agreed to sit back to back during sessions. After only a short time, this arrangement was no longer needed, but the compromise seemed to return a sense of control to the client and this freed her to participate.

Some counselors are able to tease or use humor to break impasses in counseling. Others can use informal chit-chat about baseball, the weather, or the latest trends in music as a method of lightening the tension. Still others sit in silence until somebody becomes uncomfortable and talks. As long as these tactics are not used to excess, they are acceptable; but they should never become a way to avoid the real work of counseling.

Another technique sometimes useful in working with involuntarily referred clients is to gently bait them into talking by speculating that they must have known their actions would result in their predicament, or at least that any sensible person would have known. With young offenders the counselor might say, "Do you mean to tell me you didn't know you'd get caught eventually for this? Why, I'd think there must be something wrong with somebody who doesn't realize that."

But such attempts to provoke clients must not be done in an insulting manner. Rather, they should leave the door open for the clients to try to convince the counselor that they did know better or to defend themselves in some way. Moreover, counselors must learn to recognize when their own feelings incorporate anger or irritation; feelings that, if present, will create an adversarial relationship. The goal in most cases is just to get the client talking to someone who might become an ally. The client perceives that the counselor may be an ally when the counselor actively listens and seems to care. This does not mean counselors cannot be slightly provocative or challenging.

Erickson (1980) used a technique of prescribing the symptom, thus defining the client's uncooperativeness as being under his control, not the client's. We used this technique with a hospitalized adolescent who wouldn't stay in the room for counseling by going to his room and asking him to leave while we talked about him. In groups we sometimes tell adolescents who are falling asleep that we have cast a spell over them to make them drowsy. Even when they rationally know this is not true, they still seem bothered by the assertion that we control their behavior, and they argue with us about it. Of course, in doing so they wake up and get involved, which is what we wanted. This technique is similar to interpreting resistance as cooperation. For example, a client who is struggling to find a way to escape treatment is told that this behavior is expected and in fact only ensnares the client deeper in therapy, like an animal that only becomes more tangled up as it fights to get out of the net.

Though these techniques sometimes work, they should not be overused, in fact, they should be used as a last resort to simpler strategies. But when all else fails, at least experiment and have some fun. It's much better than getting mad. Such tricks and techniques should not, however, substitute for reasonable efforts to establish empathy.

HOW TO DEVELOP EMPATHY WITH INVOLUNTARY CLIENTS

Empathy is one of the core conditions of successful counseling; indeed, it facilitates all human relationships. Counselors must have the ability to understand their clients' thoughts and feelings, but clients must also perceive the counselor's empathy. Ivey (1983) defined empathy as "experiencing the client's world as if you were the client" and described in detail counselor responses such as reflecting affect and meaning as a method of communicating empathy.

It is assumed that readers will already have mastered basic counseling skills such as those outlined by Ivey, which are highly similar to listening skills taught in Gordon's Parent Effectiveness Training and in other communications skills courses. The problem we are faced with is how to develop empathy toward clients who appear belligerent, rebellious, strange, immoral, or generally unlikable.

Involuntary clients frequently come from poor socioeconomic classes, minority populations, or criminal offender groups. It is harder for many counselors who are educated and of higher socioeconomic status to relate to members of these groups than to a sample of clients from a college counseling center. The more unlike us our clients are, the more difficult counseling becomes.

Is it realistic to expect counselors to be able to put themselves into the place of a rapist, drug dealer, spouse abuser, alcoholic, or pedophile? Can a counselor truly remain nonjudgmental about these clients? In all probability most counselors experience some sort of dislike or revulsion toward many involuntary clients. Most counselors are not able to, nor should they, abandon their values and feelings. Counselors of all colors may have prejudices and may begin to feel guilty and uncomfortable as they discover that they do have strong negative feelings about welfare mothers, unemployment recipients, or criminals.

Some counselor educators suggest that trainees try to separate people from their behaviors; dislike the behavior, like the person. And this might be sufficient in some cases to help counselors respond positively and appropriately to the client. But it is idealistic to expect that one can separate the action of child molestation from an overall assessment of the person who commits the act. People tend to judge others by the sum of their positive and negative behaviors, and highly deviant behaviors strongly influence the final assessment.

Counselors take pride in being empathic, nonjudgmental, and accepting in interpersonal relationships. Many also deny their strong feelings of anger at and rejection of clients who represent different value systems and ways of behaving. Beginning counselors in agencies and institutions frequently start their careers with rosy optimism and a love of people. This veneer is stripped as the day-to-day grind of work takes its toll. Clients are difficult, and working conditions are often poor. Burnout then ensues. How much less stressful it would be if workers could realistically and honestly confront their own view of human nature.

Counselors need to acknowledge their own values, prejudices, biases, and intolerant attitudes. They need to recognize not just the potential in themselves for selfishness or indifference to others, but they also need to acknowledge that there are many occasions when they do not feel and act as they think they should. They must accept this fact about themselves before they can presume to be accepting of other people.

Counselors must also be prepared to admit that there are clients who can be valued in the abstract, but who in the flesh do not elicit much concern or compassion. Will Rogers said he never met a man he didn't like. But most of us are less tolerant. It is so much easier to be empathic and accepting when you like your clients than when you recognize their worth and value only as an intellectual premise. Yet isn't it the highest of human achievements to be able to act on principle despite contradictory impulses? Counselors who are aware of their feelings are less likely to give symbolic homage to them in slips of the tongue or through confusing, contradictory body language and tone of voice.

Empathy and nonjudgmental attitudes are ideals, but it is a mistake to think that one either possesses them or does not. These qualities are on a continuum, and even small amounts of understanding may be enough to get counseling started or work with some problem. If counselors feel strong anger or rejection of a client, they should probably try to refer the client elsewhere. If there are moderate levels of these feelings, there are several things to do. First, counselors should spend some time processing their reactions; try to think the case through. What specifically has caused the reaction, and what can be done to control the repercussions from it?

Second, counselors should talk to another counselor to sort out their feelings. This does not have to be a full-scale consultation to be effective; just a little support can sometimes turn the tide.

Third, counselors should try to identify some of the client's positive features or strengths, which, when exposed, may improve the tone of the relationship.

Fourth, it may sometimes be helpful for counselors to share their reactions with the client, particularly if referral is being considered. The client probably senses the feelings anyway. Clinical judgment is necessary here because the point is not to unload on the client or to use the client as a counselor, but rather to admit problems in a developing relationship in an attempt to find solutions and a way to work together. Arcaya (1978) recommended self-disclosure of feelings, experiences, and thoughts as a way of building trust with the involuntary client. However, it is important not to limit these disclosures to negative reactions.

Fifth, counselors should recognize that first impressions often change. We frequently find that we come to like people the more we learn about them and as their personalities unfold before us. The more we understand, the more we are able to forgive or at least to set aside another person's faults.

Sixth, it may be helpful to be a reporter before trying to be a counselor. The counselor can approach the client by gathering information as a writer or journalist would to prepare a story. This method provides a certain detachment that suspends judgment temporarily. Instead of trying to force the unconscious to be positive toward the client, the conscious mind merely asks for a temporary reprieve. By the time the facts are in, even the "unconscious" may be more tolerant.

Finally, it should be recognized that complete empathy may be as undesirable as it is impossible to achieve. Consider that many involuntary clients come from substance abuser groups. Substance abuse counselors often are recovered alcoholics or drug users themselves, who have gone into counseling perhaps because of the belief that only an abuser can understand another abuser. Though there may be truth in this belief, it can also be argued that a person with alcoholism needs to be exposed to someone who never has had the urge to drink to excess. It could be a good experience for a substance abuser to learn that some people do not and never have structured their lives around drinking or drugs. The benefit of counseling may not always derive from being understood but from striving to understand. It is a two way street between counselor and client. When counselor and client are quite similar, they identify, not empathize, with each other. Differences between counselor and client demand a striving for empathy while they also make that empathy more difficult to attain.

A sometimes puzzling aspect of empathy is that people usually have ambivalent and conflicting feelings about issues and change, so it becomes difficult to know which side of the ambivalence to reflect to the client. For example, many alcoholics openly express a deep desire to change, to quit drinking. The counselor could respond to such expressions by empathizing with those desires. ("You feel eager to change and hopeful that you can, etc.") The alcoholic will likely respond affirmatively to these comments, but return quickly to drinking.

A different way to approach the client empathically is to reflect the hidden side of the ambivalence; to empathize with the fear of change. ("You are eager to change, but you're afraid that if you do stay sober you won't be able to stand your spouse and you'll have a divorce.") Often when the counselor empathizes with the hidden side of the client's ambivalence, a more complete picture of the client's situation unfolds than when focusing only on what is verbalized. The client probably expects the counselor to encourage change and therefore is surprised when the counselor instead understands the difficulties involved in changing.

When clients, on the other hand, wallow in self-pity and verbalize how difficult it would be to change, the counselor is likely to get an argument by emphasizing the hidden desire to do things differently. Such tactics usually result in the familiar 'yes, but' game outlined by Berne (1964): The more the counselor emphasizes the client's desire to change (and offers suggestions for how to do so), the more the client will respond by saying "Yes, but..." then repeating the objections to change. Empathy in this case is better directed to exaggerating the client's fear of change, which then paradoxically allows the client's desire for change to emerge (Frankl, 1960). So the counselor plays a 'but, yes' game with the client by anticipating and exaggerating all possible objections and feelings about changing. By verbalizing these to the client, the client then begins to say, "But while all you say is true about the problems I'll face if I change, here are the problems I'll face if I don't."

Consider also the client who doesn't want to engage in counseling. A frequent counseling approach is to logically and analytically explore the situation, map out the options and consequences for cooperating or not cooperating, then leave it to the client to rationally choose which to do. An alternative is to empathize with the client's reluctance and exaggerate it. ("Yes, you resent being forced into counseling. You're worried that I'll program you like a computer and take your choice away from you.") Most clients will deny that this is possible. The counselor can then respond by initiating a realistic discussion about the effects of counseling, having at least articulated the irrational but unexpressed fear that counseling will destroy the client's autonomy and therefore self-respect.

Counseling with involuntary clients will inevitably pose problems in the development of empathy because of one crucial difference between counselor and client: one chooses to be there, the other does not. In his book, *A Day in the Life of Ivan Denisovich* (1963), Alexander Solzhenitseyn asked whether a guard could understand the inmate in the Soviet concentration camp—because how can a man who is warm understand a man who is cold?

In counseling the involuntary client, the counselor above all else must try to understand the loss of human dignity that accompanies any type of coercion. Ironically, clients who chafe at the involuntary nature of their positions may be showing the noblest aspiration of the human spirit: the desire to be free and self-determining. Counselors can value this spirit in their clients and show positive regard for it, while also recognizing that there are inevitable limits to freedom and responsibilities that accompany the exercise of these freedoms. In the struggle to learn this lesson, counselors are very much like their clients. It is important, however, to recognize that the values of some clients are destructive and that their desire to be unfettered comes at others' expense. There is a difference between the desire to be free and the desire to be free of consequences.

WHEN CLIENTS DENY THE VALUE OF COUNSELING

The involuntary client frequently avoids participating in counseling by denying or criticizing the value of counseling to solve problems.

Some clients will disdain the counselor who seems to them to be all talk and no action. These clients have never experienced the value of reflective thought as a means of choosing a behavior. These action-oriented people put little stock in reflective thinking. Talk is also devalued by people who have experienced numerous broken promises by parents, thus negating any dependable connection between words and deeds. It is important to follow up on promises with these clients, even minor ones, such as an offer to bring a book or article to the next session. The counselor needs to establish that there can be consistent and dependable connections between words and deeds.

Many people believe that talk is cheap and useless because it cannot help them solve problems they perceive as externally caused. A client may say, "This is all word games. What is talk going to do to help get my probation officer off my back?" or, "I don't want to sit around and talk. It won't help me get the money I need for my family. Can you really do anything to help me get some money?"

Counselors need to recognize the truth in these criticisms, which emphasize the limitations rather than the strengths of counseling. Counseling cannot solve problems like discrimination and the economic punishment that goes with it. Counseling can help people choose how they want to respond to discrimination and how to take advantage of what economic resources may be available. But people who feel victimized by society see their problems as caused by circumstances outside themselves. Thus, counseling, which seeks personal change, is viewed as valueless because it is society that needs changing. The veracity of this belief is viewed to the exclusion of other truths about the power of personal initiative and action.

Therapists sometimes deny the real obstacles blocking their clients' progress, naively clinging to the Horatio Alger counseling method, which holds that hard work and persistence will always prevail over troubles. But there are circumstances that are beyond anyone's control, that no one can be held responsible for. And counselors should recognize that some clients are truly dealing with basic survival needs. Analysis of higher order needs such as self-esteem, which are usually the material of counseling, will not be applicable or helpful topics. People do not want to talk about the need for belonging when their stomachs are grumbling from hunger.

On the other hand, people often incorrectly attribute power and control to external forces and underestimate their own ability to solve problems through examining psychological processes. Alibis, excuses, and rationalizations are examples of the belief that the locus of control is external to self.

Denying the value of counseling is one way of underestimating, and therefore abdicating, personal responsibility. The counselor's difficulty is determining when the client is not appropriately assuming personal responsibility—very much a judgment call subject to opposing interpretations. Counselors must strive to make a realistic appraisal of clients' abilities to affect their situations through personal change given limitations in the environment, and also to gauge the client's degree of willingness and ability to assume responsibility by transforming talk into behavior. Ultimately, that transformation is what makes counseling worthwhile, but clients who talk the good game but do not follow through are showing a form of resistance that must be dealt with. Pointing out inconsistencies between words and deeds is the most direct technique of making a client aware of inconsistency. However, if done harshly and judgmentally, clients become even more defensive.

Ultimately, clients must scrutinize their beliefs about how much choice they have in regard to their behavior. In the meantime, a technique that can be helpful is to have clients practice assuming responsibility for everything by asking them to accept any criticism given and offer an apology, no matter how ridiculous the accusation. It is important, however, that the client attentively listen for the grain of truth in the criticism rather than just learn the language to deflect the attack. The effect of this is to help clients see that they can take criticism and survive intact. As long as self-concept is threatened, clients will externalize blame rather than take responsibility. Some assertiveness training courses instruct clients to agree with criticism by acknowledging the grain of truth in them. For example, if the counselor says the client's shoes are ugly, the client says, "You may be right." This is a simple but useful technique.

Counselors frequently respond defensively to clients' criticisms of the counseling process. This reaction may occur for several reasons. As just mentioned, clients may correctly perceive that counseling can do little to solve their immediate problems. Counseling might help develop an understanding of how the problems evolved or how they might be prevented in the future, but a person in jail wants to know only how to get out; other matters are of little immediate interest. Counselors are defensive because their skills are devalued in the face of the need the client perceives: to get released from jail. Just as the client needs to learn to accept criticism, counselors need to acknowledge the merit in the client's criticism of counseling.

Counselors also may be sensitive to criticism because they recognize that their skills can do little to correct major social problems that impinge upon the client, such as changing the unemployment statistics. A well-counseled client cannot find a job that does not exist.

Counselors themselves sometimes doubt the value of counseling and thus respond defensively to criticisms that generate self-doubt about their effectiveness even in the best of circumstances. A diplomate of the American Board of Professional Psychologists once remarked that he felt like a thief in his private practice for taking money from clients to talk about their problems. Counselors sometime feel like charlatans when they try to explain why they don't give advice ("I can't decide for you; you have to decide for yourself.") Of course, clients perceive this as a cop-out and respond by saying that if they have to decide for themselves, then what good is counseling anyway? The value of counseling is difficult to explain and even prove experimentally, and the counselor's primary affirmation of the merits of counseling comes from appreciative clients. Consequently, clients who challenge the value of counseling question the worth of the counselor's contribution.

Counselors must come to accept that theirs is a limited role. Counselors cannot dole out money, change society, or create trust by making good on promises previously broken. They can offer concrete, tangible solutions to only a few problems. Counseling usually works indirectly by helping people learn to help themselves and to make better decisions by perceiving their options

ALTERNATIVES FOR HELPING THE INVOLUNTARY CLIENT	
Beginning Approach	Method for Responding to Reluctance to Engage in Counseling
EMOTIVE	Be empathic with feelings clients have about being coerced: resentment, anger, helplessness, etc.
COGNITIVE	Challenge clients' beliefs that they have absolutely no choice and that no one should ever be pressured into doing things.
STRATEGIC	1. Amplify and exaggerate clients' feelings or beliefs for paradoxical effect 2. Reframe reluctance to enter counseling as normal and expected 3. Prescribe symptoms of reluctance
OPTIONS/ CONSEQUENCES	Explore clients' options to counseling and consequences for failure to participate.
DEFINITIONAL	Clarify counselor and client roles to define areas of choice and latitude, disassociate counselor from coercion, and establish mutually acceptable goals.

more clearly. This role is abstract and not easily explained to eager clients, much less those who have been ordered into counseling.

Although new clients are most likely to complain that counseling is just talk, many long-term clients also denigrate the process. When clients persist in these statements, it may be a sign that the issue was not dealt with conclusively at the beginning of treatment and will need more discussion.

How then can counselors respond to those who resist counseling by denying its value? For starters, it is important to have a well-defined role and definite expectations about what counseling can and cannot do. No one should feel guilty because of an inability to end discrimination, but all counselors should be convinced that they have a service to offer.

The most futile response to clients who devalue counseling is to try to rationally convince them of the value of the therapeutic process. It may be helpful to acknowledge the element of truth in the criticisms; to admit the limitations of counseling. Unfortunately, some therapists give up too easily and dismiss counseling as inappropriate for the client who lacks "motivation" or who is not "amenable to treatment."

When acknowledging the limitations of counseling, the counselor can also help clients explore the reasons for their feelings, thereby beginning a counseling relationship while allowing complaints about it. For example:

Client: I don't know what good this counseling will do. What I need is a job.
Counselor: Well, you're right. I can't give you a job myself. And you're pretty pessimistic that talking can help you figure out where and how to look for one.
Client: I've been looking.
Counselor: So you know all there is to know about how to get training and find jobs and you don't need to learn anything more at all?
Client: So, I suppose you are going to show me how to get a job.
Counselor: I don't know. We haven't talked enough for me to know if I know anything you don't. Why don't you tell me how you've been looking and where you've applied. Maybe we'll get some ideas.

The key element here is that the counselor did not get hooked into making unrealistic promises or acting so discouraged that counseling had to be terminated. Varga (1971) provided a thoughtful discussion of understanding motivation in "poorly motivated" clients in employment counseling. The most important point is not to assume that the client is unmotivated. Rather, attempts must be made to discover what leverage can be achieved by using the interests the client does have.

Other problems of denial

Devaluing counseling and externalizing blame are examples of a larger problem of denial; a problem that may begin in early sessions and continue throughout treatment. Denial takes many forms. A dying person may refuse to believe a diagnosis, or criminals about to be released from prison refuse to acknowledge that they may return despite the fact that they can identify no significant changes in themselves since the prison sentence was imposed.

Denial can be viewed as an intrapsychic symptom or as a systemic problem. In either case the important question is what function the denial serves. According to intrapsychic models, denial protects the conscious mind or self-esteem from unpleasant truths. In a systemic view, denial protects the status quo structure of the family or perpetuates habitual patterns of relating that are governed by tacit rules.

How the counselor deals with denial depends upon the model of counseling being used and assumptions about the mechanism at work in the denial process. A counselor working with involuntary clients needs to think about whether his client's denial is somehow different from that of voluntary clients.

The nature of almost all counseling boils down to helping clients to accept appropriate personal responsibility by choosing alternatives from among the available options. So counseling the involuntary client really is not entirely different from counseling anyone else except that the denial of responsibility is exaggerated and extreme. With the involuntary client the counselor often suspects that denial is conscious and malicious. For example, offenders may lie about their involvement in a crime, or teenagers with school problems may lie to their counselor about how much they study. Substance abusers also avoid taking responsibility for their actions by lying to their counselors, and sometimes to themselves, about their use of drugs and alcohol.

When denial is extreme and possibly willful, counselors often become irritated and begin to believe that their clients are unmotivated and therefore not amenable to treatment. Sometimes counselors handle their vexation with clients by attack and confrontation. Many confrontation techniques, such as the hot seat, are popular in drug abuse and correctional programs, but there is little evidence that they are effective (Elkin, 1984). These techniques can become dehumanizing and degrading if the real purpose is to enable the counselor to vent personal feelings in the guise of counseling. This dehumanizing behavior is more likely when the involuntary referral is seen as a different "kind" of person than the voluntary referral. To say that people are "unmotivated," as is often said of the unvoluntary client, is to strip them of their humanity since there is really no such condition in a living person; anyone who acts is motivated, though perhaps not in socially accepted ways. Counselors must be careful not to think of involuntary clients as different in kind from voluntary clients (West, 1975).

As a general rule, it is ineffective to try to browbeat or intimidate clients to get them to stop blaming others for their troubles. Arguing and heated discussions usually only reinforce stubbornness in a client. The keys to dealing with this kind of denial are timing and patience. Because most clients eventually have moments of vulnerability and openness to intervention, the counselor must be like a fisherman waiting for the fish to nibble at the bait. And because most change requires repetitive teaching, patience is required to deliver the message from a multitude of perspectives until the summative effect takes hold. Like a child learning to speak, many clients appear not to be absorbing any input until one day they seem to master concepts in a flash of insight. Counselors are seldom in a position to force a client to try a new behavior, but sometimes they can hint, prod, and push gently. As the saying goes, you can lead a horse to water, but you can't make him drink. But while he's at the trough, you can splash him with a little water.

Premature Termination

Clients who feel browbeaten or intimidated frequently terminate counseling prematurely. Pekarik (1986) showed that self-referred clients were half as likely to terminate counseling prematurely as other-referred clients. This is an important and often overlooked issue (Ward, 1984). Involuntary clients may terminate counseling prematurely for several reasons. One important reason is that they frequently do not become fully engaged in counseling because they regard counseling as merely a fixed number of sessions to endure. If this is the case, reflecting upon strategies for effective termination is of little value; the counselor would be better advised to spend time examining what could have been done to make the counseling more meaningful in the first place.

Involuntary clients may be expected to be especially reactive and sensitive to the inevitable trials and tribulations of counseling. Forced clients may be hypersensitive to perceived coercion and consequently may abruptly and unexpectedly terminate, or simply not reappear for sessions. On the other hand, many involuntary clients with antisocial or dys-social tendencies may not form a bond with the counselor in counseling and therefore will not experience the expected grief and mourning other clients (and counselors) feel as the counseling relationship ends. Hence quitting counseling is easy for them to do.

As Ward (1984) suggested, it is important to try to figure out with clients, particularly prematurely terminating clients, their reasons for and feelings about terminating. This process is important because it may help the client resume counseling at a later date with the counselor or another counselor. Sometimes the client's attempts at premature termination point to resistance or problems in counseling that were obstructing change. Timely identification and intervention may clarify these issues so that counseling can continue.

RESISTANCE TO INITIATING THERAPY: A CASE IN POINT

Contrasting styles of meeting resistance may become clearer by examining a case and alternative approaches to it. Basch (1982) gave a condensed account of the initial interview of a case and a succinct summary of his feelings about the dialogue. As he noted, other therapists might have handled the situation differently but just as effectively. As Basch also commented, the most frustrating case is one in which the client resists examining the resistance and gets into an interpersonal struggle with the counselor.

The person in the case reported was clearly resistant. Though the client sought out the therapist, it was not for therapy but for advice about what to do about his children. Thus, he in no way accepted responsibility for his difficulties and bridled when the therapist suggested he had some problems.

The patient, Mr. Adam Hoheit, is a forty-five-year-old investment banker. His bearing and appearance radiate success and authority. The following is a condensed account of the first interview.

Therapist: (walking into the waiting room and offering his hand) Mr. Hoheit? I am Dr. Basch.

Mr. Hoheit: (indifferently shaking the proffered hand) I have to be out of here by 2:00 and you are five minutes late, doctor.

Therapist: Come in please.

Mr. Hoheit: (settling down in the designated chair) Will we be done by 2:00, doctor? I have a meeting by 2:15.

Therapist: Will we be done with what?

Mr. Hoheit: Right. I guess you don't even know what I'm here for. Actually it shouldn't take too long. Abner Tatum was your patient and he is my client. We were talking at lunch the other day and I mentioned my problem to him. Abner said he wanted to stay out of it, but he said you had been of great help to him during his divorce, so I thought perhaps I could use some of your counsel in my circumstances too.

Therapist: I'd be glad to be of help if I can.

Mr. Hoheit: It's not really for me. I need advice regarding my children. I want to know whether, in your professional opinion, my getting a divorce from my wife will hurt them. I have a boy age five, and two daughters, sixteen and fourteen. The two older ones will be leaving home to go to college fairly soon anyway, but the five-year-old worries me a little.

Therapist: I don't think that's a question I can answer. If you'll tell me about your situation I may be able to clarify your thinking.

Mr. Hoheit: You mean if I can give you more information about him then you can tell me how my boy will be affected? I suppose it does differ with each personality.

Therapist: No. I would like to hear from you about your children, their personalities, and the effects you think a divorce will have on them because that will help me get a better picture of what's going on with you.

Mr. Hoheit: All this will take a long time. I have to be out of here by 2:00 you know.

Therapist: There is no telling how long it will take. If there is reason to meet more than once I'm prepared to do so.

Mr. Hoheit: (with a sneer on his face and a sarcastic tone) Sounds to me like you're trying to set up something for yourself, doctor.

Therapist: Please explain yourself.

Mr. Hoheit: Well, I asked you a simple question. I came to get a professional opinion from you as I would from a dentist, a lawyer, or a surgeon. I'm perfectly willing to pay what it costs to get it, but you are already making me into a client or a patient—whatever you people call it—and I'm just telling you before we go any further that I just might not care for that idea. What do you say to that?

Therapist: First of all, the question you asked me is not, as you suggest, a simple one. Moreover, as I told you, it is impossible to answer it as you asked it. I am willing to believe that you didn't know that and I could understand your disappointment at being told that it was so. However, what I'd like you to explain is the tone of your voice and the look on your face when you said I was "trying to set something up" for

myself. It sounded cynical and sarcastic. As if there was something dirty going on here. It seemed to me as if your initial purpose in coming here was forgotten and your goal was not to enlist my help but to make me feel guilty and ashamed. For some reason you felt a need to attack me.
Mr. Hoheit: (silence)
Therapist: Well?
Mr. Hoheit: You and my wife.
Therapist: Hmm.
Mr. Hoheit: That's what she complains about. (in a falsetto voice) "You're attacking me." "You're continually undermining me." "I love you, but if I am going to retain my sanity I have to leave you, Adam." Silly damned nonsense.
Therapist: You mean it's your wife who is leaving you? I was under the impression that you were going to seek a divorce.
Mr. Hoheit: What's the difference who is leaving whom! It's the boy I'm concerned about.
Therapist: It sounds to me as if you are in a lot of trouble with yourself and that we have much more to talk about. It's getting close to the time you said you had to leave. I would suggest that we make at least two more appointments so that I may clarify your situation for myself and make my recommendations.
Mr. Hoheit: So you think I need therapy?
Therapist: There's very little doubt in my mind about that. The question is whether or not you can lend yourself to that process and, if so, what form it should take.
Mr. Hoheit: Listen, the people I'm supposed to meet with aren't that important. I can let them wait if you have the time to go on.
Therapist: I did have more time allotted for this first meeting, but I wouldn't feel comfortable going on knowing that I was willfully inconveniencing the people waiting for you. How long will your meeting take?
Mr. Hoheit: An hour, maybe an hour and a half. Definitely no more.
Therapist: If you have the time I could see you later in the day.
Mr. Hoheit: I don't want to keep you.
Therapist: It's no problem. I have to stay late anyway today. Would 5:30 be okay?
Mr. Hoheit: Fine, thank you doctor.
Therapist: You're welcome. Good-bye till then, Mr. Hoheit.

This patient displays what Murray has called a narcissistic sense of entitlement. He feels perfectly justified in demanding that the world meet his needs to the exclusion of all other reality. Incensed that he was kept waiting a few minutes, he has no hesitation about inconveniencing others when he feels it is in his interest to do so. It would, of course, have been a serious mistake to indulge him in this attitude. As it turned out, Mr. Hoheit did come back, psychotherapy was recommended, and he was seen three times a week for a period of several months. He was able to gain sufficient insight into his behavior to ease the strain between himself and his wife considerably.

His need to control everyone and everything around him was roo in his fear that if he did not do so he would be seen as weak, gullible, and easily imposed on; similar to the way in which he experienced his father. None of this was, of course, evident or suspected when I first met Mr. Hoheit. I bring up this material to illustrate an extreme example of a not uncommon situation in which the patient's fear that the therapist will not be strong enough to withstand the onslaught of the patient's needs leads him to wrestle the therapist from the very first meeting or telephone call for control of the therapeutic situation, hoping against hope all the while that the doctor will not be intimidated. Since at that point therapy has not yet begun there is no basis for dealing with the potential patient's behavior by interpretation. Attempts to placate the patient are seen by him as weakness on the part of the therapist and may well frighten him into finding some pretext for not returning.

It was most instructive for me to see that after the first few encounters with this patient, in which I apparently proved to him that I had the requisite strength to deal with him, the resistance to treatment dissipated and did not present a problem in the years we subsequently worked together. There was, of course, the expected intrapsychic resistance to uncovering aspects of repressed and disavowed memories, feelings, and motives, but it was clear to both of us that the struggle was within him and not with me.

There are many different ways in which patients who need to do so attempt to dominate the therapist. Mr. Hoheit is presented only as a dramatic illustration of what often confronts us in a more subtle and disguised form. Nor am I advocating my approach to this particular patient as paradigmatic. Another therapist might have handled the situation differently but equally effectively. This particular clinical example is only given to illustrate that when a patient's resistance takes the form of acting out the question "Who is in control here?" it behooves the therapist to respond, in whatever way is congenial to his personality, "I am."*

An important disagreement to Basch's approach stems from the question of who should be in control in counseling (therapy); the counselor or the client. Basch answers, the counselor. A different view is that the counselor should be in charge of himself or herself while not challenging the client's autonomy either. That is, each person is in charge only of him or herself. Basch was correct in not allowing himself to be manipulated into extending the session, an extension which he knew would have inconvenienced others. But was it unnecessarily antagonistic to confront Mr. Hoheit by telling him that his tone of voice was cynical, sarcastic, and attacking? True though this may have been, many clients might become even more defensive and angry.

---

*Basch, M. "Dynamic Psychotherapy and its Frustrations." In *Resistance: Psychodynamic and Behavioral Approaches,* edited by P. Wachtel. New York: Plenum Press, 1982. Used with permission.

The traditional method of dealing with resistance is to confront it by pointing out how it manifests itself. Then, the resistance is clarified by examining what motivates it. Next, the deep roots are interpreted. And, finally, the working through occurs over the course of therapy by repetition of the confrontation, clarification, and interpretation (Strean, 1985). But there are other views on how to deal with resistance in counseling.

It is necessary for counselors not to compromise themselves, but perhaps it is not important to establish control through confrontation. Counselors can quietly act on their own values without implying to others that theirs are wrong.

Perhaps most important, counselors need not articulate their view that the client needs therapy. The realization of this is the client's ultimate responsibility. Most people reject being told that they are sick or wrong, so announcing it serves little purpose and may impede clients' confronting their deficiencies honestly. As long as clients have an external adversary they can avoid an internal scrutiny.

Premature confrontation of such clients may result not in self-examination but in development of a symmetrical, escalating struggle for control between counselor and client. Basch was successful with Mr. Hoheit, but other clients may have prematurely terminated counseling. Mental health center records are filled with charts of clients who come once and depart angrily with the counselor's notes suggesting that the client was not amenable to counseling.

The issue of whether and how to confront resistance is difficult to settle. The only thing that is clear is that counselors should not confront to ventilate and make themselves feel better or to satisfy their own needs. Ellis (1985), typically known for forcefully disputing irrational beliefs through logic and persuasion, commented that when clients resist because they doubt your point, then argue expertly with them. But when they resist because they don't like therapy in general, it is important to be personable and to build the relationship. Ellis also acknowledged that there are confrontation styles that are more indirect and easygoing and less direct and hard-nosed. The indirect method couples empathic reflection with questioning to lead to a point rather than direct disagreements and challenges. For example, the counselor might say, "What did that behavior get for you?" rather than, "Your action only succeeded in making your predicament worse; apparently you persist in believing you shouldn't have to work hard at finding the solution for this problem."

Miller (1985) pointed out that confrontation is often used with alcoholics to break down denial but that much research points to the destructive impact of counselor hostility on therapy, hostility often perceived during confrontation. Too much confrontation seems to arouse anxiety but also triggers self-defense rather than coping and problem-solving behaviors. Miller also highlighted research showing how feedback about discrepancy between actual and ideal self could be used in confrontation if coupled with feedback about improvement when the counseling process develops attainable and specific goals for the client to try to meet.

Miller's central and well-taken point is that low motivation is usually seen by counselors as a client characteristic, when a more useful view is to see motivation as a complex interaction of factors, including therapist characteristics. Another point he made is that verbalized resistance to participating in counseling has little empirical correlation with actual participation or with treatment outcome. Counselors usually define the motivated client as one who is distressed, accepts the therapist's point of view and complies. But as Ellis (1985) demonstrated, sometimes a client quite correctly and rationally decides the counselor is off the mark with a particular interpretation or can't help for other reasons and, therefore, rationally resists.

Bratter (1974) presented a compelling account of the development of his personal style with addicts, and he strongly argued the need for intense involvement with and confrontation of "unmotivated" clients. Like Ellis, he seems to have the ability to confront without appearing not to care, and as long as clients perceive the caring, they probably will not react as intensely with denial or other forms of resistance. (It's quite possible that addicts in Bratter's case and New Yorkers in Ellis' case can understand confrontation better than small-town or rural clients). Forrest (1982) offered a thoughtful discussion of confrontation with the alchoholic whose denial impedes progress. However, the research on this subject is sparse.

Until there is more research on confrontation techniques, our preference would be this: First, the counselor should assess the client's capacity to form a relationship and bond with the counselor. Clients who can form a therapeutic alliance through empathy should be helped to do so. Some clients may not form this alliance unless the counselor brings the issue into the open by talking about the client's inability to trust or relate. Other clients (antisocial personalities) may lack the capacity to form relationships, so counseling cannot proceed with this as a foundation.

Second, when the relationship is reasonably secure, it should be able to withstand indirect questioning about beliefs underlying resistance to counseling, such as, "I shouldn't be forced into treatment; I don't have a problem," or "Counseling can't help my kind of problem." If these low-key measures don't work, the counselor can always use a more vigorous, forceful challenge to the client's resistance to counseling.

Third, when the reluctant client has been engaged in a counseling process, other resistances to change will appear as with any client. The counselor will have to decide how to deal with that resistance. The choices are many: looking for and disputing irrational beliefs; exploring feelings associated with the resistance; using paradox and other techniques recommended by various counseling approaches.

Another approach to dealing with the resistant, abrasive client was demonstrated by Erickson (1980), whose skills are probably beyond replication by most of us. Nevertheless, his policy clearly was to meet patients' needs but on terms they proposed. He believed the therapist must develop keen sensitivity to patients' inner processes so that they can meet their problems by use of already acquired learning. Though Erickson may have appeared at times to be as abrasive as his patients, he was never adversarial, and viewed the patient's attack as a symptom whose power could be used by the therapist to help the patient.

Having looked at involuntary clients from a variety of perspectives, we can offer a few preliminary suggestions about entering counseling with them.

1. The first step is to build a relationship and join with the client if possible. The counselor accomplishes this by empathizing with the feelings associated with coercion, such as anger, fear of loss of control, embarrassment, etc. The counselor may also disassociate him or herself from the source of coercion. Explore with the client the consequences for failure to participate in counseling, begin to define the nature of the counseling process, and clarify mutual expectations.

2. Bring into the open, question, and challenge (subtly or directly, depending on the counselor's style) the thinking that lies behind the client's reluctance to participate. Usually the client may believe that he or she shouldn't be forced into doing things or that there isn't a problem to be worked on in counseling.

3. Try to find a problem, however small, that the client can agree to work on. Establish attainable goals.

4. Show interest in the client and express a sincere desire to help. Schedule the next appointment quickly to avoid too much time between visits. Don't expect the client to cave in, confess sins, and express appreciation. Clients often continue to verbalize resistance to counseling while beginning to cooperate.

5. Complete an assessment and treatment plan of the client's problems. Pay special attention to anticipated resistances stemming from involuntary entrance into counseling. Conceptualize how you see the client's resistance from the counseling model you use. Decide how you will respond to resistance: Through confrontation of irrational beliefs? Through exploring feelings? Through interpretation of the deep roots of the client's resistance, or a systemic analysis and/or paradoxical techniques?

Once past the beginning session or two, whether working in an institution or not, counselors will begin to use whatever frame of reference they are most comfortable with, be it a person-centered reality therapy, psychodynamic, or family systems approach. Resistance will be interpreted according to that frame of reference. Nevertheless, there are several principles of counseling reluctant clients that apply regardless of theoretical orientation.

7

Principles of Working with Involuntary Clients

Chapter Seven

Every counselor wishes that there were a magic wand to wave and a magic word to say that would demolish their clients' defenses and leave them open to constructive counseling. But no such wands or words exist. The challenge is to explore ideas in such a way as to engage reluctant clients in counseling, keep them working, and prevent their premature termination by following a few common sense principles.

The voluntary client typically enters counseling and has good rapport with the counselor for a period of time. Then, the ambivalence about the desire to change emerges and the first treatment crisis occurs (Strean, 1985). The involuntary client begins with a treatment crisis and enters a series of rapids which threaten to throw both counselor and client out of the life raft. It must be constantly kept in mind that resistance to change is expected and that all people entering therapy have a certain resentment to being there and ambivalence about whether to change. Clients' reasons for being reluctant in counseling are quite different, as are their styles of acting on their reluctance.

PROVIDING STRUCTURE: SETTING EXPECTATIONS

A client intent upon subverting the counseling process can do so regardless of how explicit the counselor has been about such matters as appointment time, conduct in sessions, and objectives of sessions. Nevertheless, being clear about such things is necessary if for no other reason than to help counselors decide whether the client's behavior is due to resistance or simple misunderstanding. Hesitation and uncertainty are frequently damaging when dealing with difficult clients. It is always important at least to try to get clients to discuss their expectations, though this effort may be futile. Many clients cannot articulate their expectations or may choose to hide them if they are negative.

Contracts between clients and counselors are sometimes helpful, but some clients are as adept as lawyers at twisting or distorting written agreements. The contract should be looked at as a communication aid or teaching device, not a binding document. Writing down goals of treatment, homework assignments, and other agreements about who will do what and when can help clarify details that often unintentionally remain murky. The counselor should avoid getting into an emotional struggle with clients who do not fulfill terms of the contract, however. These struggles are seldom successful in getting clients to admit their errors and make genuine change.

Above all else, counselors must make clear to the client what they are and are not willing to tolerate. Institutional or agency rules and regulations should be studied carefully and followed. If a rule is pointless or harmful, proper administrative channels should be followed to change it, but counselors should not arbitrarily allow rules to be broken. The more precisely counselors define in their own minds what they expect, the more able clients will be to choose to meet those expectations or violate them. Then whatever decisions are made will have a clear basis (Goodyear and Bradley, 1980). Strean (1985), however, stated that trying to get all the ground rules clarified in the first session was unnecessary and often detrimental because doing so could give the impression that the therapist was mainly interested in getting down the rules and not in helping the client.

MAXIMIZING CHOICE, MINIMIZING DEMAND

Few clients, or therapists for that matter, can directly face all their shortcomings without getting defensive. No one (except a martyr perhaps) likes drudgery or pain. Most people like to feel as though they have some control and choice over what is happening to them. Consequently, any counseling process that begins with an exhaustive listing of what is wrong with the client will likely be met with defensive resistance. If the counselor explains that such serious problems can only be solved with intensive and extensive work, many clients will give up in despair or will quite understandably look for a way to avoid all that agony.

The counselor may try to defuse some of this reluctance by suggesting that the sessions "will lead wherever they lead and take as long as they take." Instead of making a series of appointments all at once, schedules can sometimes be set a week at a time. The counselor can try to offer a selection of times to the client. If homework is to be assigned, it should be manageable and nonthreatening, to establish a pattern of compliance and success.

Especially with children, and perhaps with adults as well, counselors can try to make the experience enjoyable through art or games. Counselors should eliminate, as much as possible, annoying forms and bureaucratic obstacles. They should minimize waits and in general make counseling as easy as possible to begin. Clients who do not want to be in counseling to begin with do not need to be given reasons to complain about the process.

Most counselors have a view of the importance of counseling that exceeds the client's estimation. There is no point in feeling defensive about such an attitude in a client. Only time will tell whether the client will benefit from a therapeutic process anyway. Counselors need to recognize that, for a variety of reasons, many people dismiss counseling as a relatively unimportant, ineffective process. Counselors are viewed by some as intruders into private affairs. Such opinions cannot be changed by mere protestation. So it is important to respect clients' views and allow them to have their opinions.

Many counselors try to minimize demand by reducing or eliminating the financial cost of counseling for the client. Though fees are not an issue for counselors in many institutional settings, they are in private practices. Traditionally, one measure of resistance is whether the client pays the bill. But in reality few clients in private counseling these days are totally responsible for the cost of services since insurance, government programs, or parents pay for the service. This deferral to third-party payment separates the client from direct responsibility for the counseling. (The more society arranges to pay the bill, the greater the argument that it is society that wants the person to change and not the person himself.) In any event, it is a mistake to make counseling too cheap. Clients who are court ordered into treatment should pay for the services as they are able. The counselor should be able to negotiate a fair arrangement on fees as on any other aspect of counseling but should not become a martyr to help someone else in need (Menninger, 1958; Strean, 1985).

SAVING FACE

The act of entering counseling is still embarrassing to many clients, especially when the referral has been mandated by a third party. For many, entering counseling signifies loss of control and arouses fears of dependency. In such circumstances, many clients will enter counseling angrily and will identify the counselor with the authority who ordered the counseling, i.e., the judge or welfare official. The counselor needs to recognize the source of this wrath from the beginning and defuse it, perhaps saving face for both parties.

Empathizing with the client's feelings of being coerced is perhaps the best thing to try first. But disassociating oneself from the referral source may also be helpful. For example, a counselor who takes court referrals of men who batter their wives may emphasize that, though the court made the referral, the court will have no right to interfere in the conduct of counseling sessions. Thus, a subtle distinction between courts and counselors is made, along with the suggestion that the client's desires are important in determining how sessions will be conducted. This returns a sense of control and dignity to the client. Of course, the counselor must take care not to side with the client against the referral source, as that can lead to an unhealthy misidentification of values and positions.

Another tactic is to refrain from identifying the counseling sessions as such, and instead to call them meetings or briefings for the purpose of "filling the counselor in on details;" the less threatening the label the better. Many people are leery of counselors and other assorted "shrinks." In some circles going to therapy is high in status; for other people it is perceived as an insult. Changing the name of the process may be helpful in getting things started.

Relabeling other things may also reduce resistance in the involuntary client. Instead of calling a client's beliefs irrational, it may be less offensive to say they are controversial and subject to discussion. Then, a cognitively oriented therapist can start the discussion to examine the beliefs.

IGNORING RESISTANCE OR NOT TAKING THE BAIT

There are many things said or done in counseling that would have been better left untouched. For example, if a client in an institutional setting inappropriately attempts to form a special alliance with a counselor by gossiping about another staff member, the best tactic initially may be to change the subject rather than deal directly with the gossip—as long as the remark is mild and unlikely to cause any material consequences. Ignoring the client in this instance may allow time to establish a better relationship that would withstand the tension of a more direct discussion of the inappropriateness of a similar remark later. Timing is critical. It may also be appropriate to suggest that the client talk directly with the staff member. If the counselor offers to set up a three way meeting to explore the complaint, most clients will quickly decline and stop complaining.

Angry or blaming remarks from clients can also frequently be ignored. Counselors will have different beliefs and approaches to this, some preferring to deal with such problems as they arise. Particularly at the beginning of counseling, direct discussion of how the client is externalizing blame may result in the client feeling blamed. Some clients may test their counselors by telling fabricated, exaggerated stories to get shock reactions and to determine whether the counselor will maintain confidentiality. If the story becomes known to other staff members, the client knows exactly who passed it on.

Regardless of whether the client's reason is to see whether the counselor is judgmental or trustworthy, counselors should take everything with a grain of salt, withholding reactions until more is known. Not taking the bait is a good strategy for avoiding premature termination of counseling because it allows clients to test the waters to see whether they want to come in. Counselors who work as part of a therapeutic team have the ethical obligation to let the client know who his or her case will be regularly discussed with.

CREATING OPTIMUM ANXIETY TO STIMULATE SELF-EXAMINATION

Counselors are trained to work with people who become aware of a problem or uncomfortable feeling and ask for therapeutic help. These clients recognize the need for change because they want to feel better or because they realize their situation or problem, if left unchanged, will bring about undesirable consequences. Although they sense something is amiss, they may blame someone else for their unhappiness, anger, or anxiety or view their unwanted situation as caused by factors outside their control. Nevertheless, they seek counseling, because they hope to find a way to make others change or because their anger seems unproductive and draining.

The involuntary client, on the other hand, often does not have anxiety or lacks awareness of it. Anger may exist but the person does not see this as inappropriate because he or she believes others are at fault. Most important, the righteousness of the anger prevents the client from considering how self-defeating the anger is, thus there is no motivation to change it.

So, clients who are referred involuntarily to counseling do not pour out their feelings or avidly enlist the counselor to help them change a bad situation. How then should the counselor proceed?

One possibility is to try to create anxiety or self-doubt in the person. One way of doing this is to confront clients by pointing out inconsistencies between their behavior and professed beliefs, or by pointing out how their choice of actions resulted in their present situation. Another method is to provide feedback of how others view and evaluate them. The stronger the relationship between counselor and client, the more likely such methods will be tolerated by and beneficial to the client.

However, many clients will reject these attempts as unwelcome criticisms, particularly people who do not develop trust easily. Clients who don't have or are unaware of the usual anxiety will also deflect these techniques. A particular danger in confronting clients before a relationship is formed is that the counselor then becomes the adversary. But clients who are involuntary do not give counseling the benefit of a few warm-up sessions, which makes it difficult to time the confrontations appropriately. There is no opportunity for a client/counselor bond to form because the client doesn't let that happen. The trick is to create the anxiety without being blamed by the client for doing so. Much of the success of doing this depends on style. Some counselors can smile while confronting their clients and the client does not link the "negative" confrontation with the "friendly" counselor. Nothing sticks to the "teflon" counselor.

While creating anxiety is often necessary, it is also true that much resistance stems from too much anxiety. Reducing anxiety, then, helps clients relax and take a more measured view of their situation. One technique for reducing anxiety is to "normalize" the problem. That is, point out how many people are in a similar situation and how it is not a great personal aberration. For example, a man may be forced into treatment by his wife, who is upset at the provocative behavior between the father and daughter. The counselor may carefully point out that many men find themselves interested in their daughters' sexual development, but there is a line between appropriate and inappropriate interest that is sometimes crossed. By saying this, the counselor empathizes with the man's criticized feelings while clearly defining acting on those feelings in sexual ways as inappropriate. The father may be relieved because he may have felt freakish and embarrassed at having feelings and fantasies he could not prevent. This reduction of anxiety then frees him to explore acceptable ways of channeling his feelings.

Still another way of reducing anxiety is to ask questions in early sessions that do not tap material that is too sensitive. Sometimes taking a family history can be fun and informative as it places the client in his or her social context. Asking a client to describe the personalities of different family members and the client's relationship to them can be revealing and is something most people can do without much prompting.

A technique related to creating anxiety is inducing frustration. Erikson (1980) described this technique as prompting a low intensity response, then inhibiting it before it could be expressed. For example, in a family meeting a reticent child might be asked a question then quickly denied the opportunity to answer by a quick change of subject. The frustration in the child builds until he or she is bursting with something to say. Gestalt therapists create a similar effect by trying to create awareness in the client without giving any indication of how that awareness should be channeled. A counselor might point out how the client is clenching his teeth but would not interpret what the clenching means. The induced awareness of the behavior brings into consciousness the client's unfinished business, which is frustrating, and the client then becomes motivated to resolve the incompletion. The counselor, refusing to take responsibility for what the behavior means, forces the client to do so (Patterson, 1980). Thus, Erikson creates tension by frustrating a response. Gestalt therapists create tension by inducing awareness of unfinished business.

Timing interventions for critical moments

Another tactic is not to try to create anxiety or discomfort, but to wait until clients are suffering as a natural consequence of their actions, such as catching alcoholics when their world is crumbling around them or criminals when the awesome reality of imprisonment seems imminent. Timing interventions this way tends to keep the counselor out of the adversarial role. Unfortunately, however, many counselors want to ease their clients' pain at these moments by offering reassurance or by enhancing their self-esteem. Instead, what is often necessary is a persistent, but not cruel, inventory of the person and assessment of the situation (Samenow, 1984).

Counselors have to learn to strike while the iron is hot by doing concentrated work while the client is open to it. Weekly sessions will fail because the client's defenses will have reconstructed between sessions. Counselors should not kick their clients while they are down, but they should not help their clients up too quickly either. The difficulty with this approach is that it is not preventive, and the client's life is already a shambles before openness to counseling occurs. By then, the crisis tends to turn counseling either to emotional exchanges or to strategizing about how to escape the immediate crisis, rather than attempting to mutually determine the roots of the problem and encouraging the client to accept personal responsibility for it.

Piquing curiosity

A difficult method of engaging reluctant clients is to intrigue them and pique their curiosity. Yochelson and Samenow (1976, 1977) describe how they give clients a lengthy description of their hunches about their behavior and thoughts about work, school, friendships, and family. The accuracy of the unflattering portrait disarms criminals who wonder how someone who does not know them knows them so well.

Another variation is to make a prediction about the client's behavior. For example, batterers whose wives have left them are usually distraught and seek counseling because their wives demand it before they will consider reconciliation. Counselors can point out that the man's motivation to continue counseling will dissipate as soon as his wife returns.

Some men are quite aware of their intent but are intrigued with the counselor's insight and conduct (assuming that the counselor has declined requests to strategize about how to get the woman to return rather than how to change the violent behavior). Other men may deny to themselves that they lack sincere interest in counseling except as a device to get their wives back, but the truth will become clear over time, and the accuracy of the earlier assessment can be pointed out later to weaken the man's self-assured certainty.

Sometimes psychological tests make clients curious and willing to talk, if for no other reason than to satisfy a curiosity about self, much like the desire to see pictures of oneself in various poses or costumes. Some clients, however, treat testing as an opportunity to manipulate or make fun of the counselor, and then the testing results must be treated with caution.

IDENTIFYING POSITIVE INTENT

People who are involuntarily referred to counseling are usually in conflict with other people, either legally or socially. When such conflict exists, parties to the conflict tend to view each other's motivations negatively. Parents who are having trouble with a rebellious child frequently say the child is being stubborn or selfish. But it is possible for the counselor to put the child's behavior in a different light and soften hostility by saying he or she is showing signs of wanting to be independent, a praiseworthy characteristic of anyone soon to become an adult. Many behaviors that are ordinarily viewed negatively are perhaps done for basically positive and human reasons. If the underlying motivation can be understood, the counselor is in a better position to be empathic and nonjudgmental towards the client, and the counseling process will be aided.

While it is important to try to look for the positive intent behind negative behaviors, counselors need to consider that such intent may not always be present. Yochelson and Samenow (1976, 1977), for example, view the motivations of the offender as egocentric and irresponsible. They describe the criminal as being interested in the excitement of criminal activity rather than in the dull pleasure of responsible life. They state that criminals view themselves as unique people who should not be subjected to the rules that govern ordinary people. The criminal was further described as one who wants power over others for personal benefit.

Yochelson and Samenow's position leaves little room for finding positive intent behind criminal activity. The correctness of their position is difficult to prove conclusively and thus will be assessed by the individual counselor according to his or her personal experience and beliefs. However, it does seem reasonable to believe, as do Yochelson and Samenow, that criminal irresponsibility is on a continuum. On one end of the continuum are basically normal people who occasionally think and act irresponsibly. On the other end are people whose values, motivations, thoughts, and behavior are largely criminal.

To the extent that involuntary clients are essentially normal and are not antisocial personalities, their problematic behavior may have positive intent at its core. A juvenile who is truant from school may be unconsciously reacting to stress by trying to attract his or her parents' attention in order to keep them from arguing between themselves. The child suffers less stress from being truant than from worrying about the parents' arguments. On the other hand, some criminal children may be truant because they are simply bored with the demands of school and prefer the excitement of street life. In order to be successful at finding positive intent, counselors need to have an understanding of their clients' underlying personality structures and interpersonal interactions. This boils down to understanding what end is served by an apparently illogical, self-damaging behavior.

Identifying positive intent in the involuntary client is a precondition for use of many powerful paradoxical techniques. Tennen et al. (1981) described defiance-based paradoxical prescriptions as successful because the client rebels against the counselor's interpretation of a positively motivated negative behavior. For example, a therapist tells a violent client with a macho self-image that he should continue to criticize his wife because doing so reveals his sensitive, emotional side. Presumably this sensitive, emotional personality exists beneath the macho exterior but is not something the client can consciously acknowledge. Thus, the negative behavior becomes restricted as the positive intent is interpreted.

But as implied earlier, perhaps the most important benefit from looking for positive intent comes from the increased empathy the counselor can feel toward the client. Clients who appear rebellious, uncooperative, angry, and uncommunicative can be viewed positively as wanting self-determination (Riordan et al., 1978). Counselors who recognize this motivation are less likely to be critical or to try to impose unnecessary restrictions on the client that would increase rebellious behavior.

Extended discussions of relabeling, reframing, and positive intent can be found in Anderson and Stewart (1983) and Watzlawick et al. (1974).

USING NONVERBAL TECHNIQUES

Another method to use when working with involuntary or difficult nonverbal clients is to engage them in physical activities, such as crafts, sports, or survival skills expeditions. People of all ages and types can learn much about themselves through involvement in survival tests. Situations that expose clients to new stimuli, such as the Scared Straight program, may also have educational value. They are especially useful because clients get caught up in the experience and find themselves participating to survive, emotionally and physically. Encounter groups using the "hot-seat" have a similar quality. Corey et al. (1982) described a variety of Gestalt-like exercises for the resistant and involuntary client in groups, and their book is a good primer for therapists interested in such techniques.

CAPITALIZING ON VARIOUS STYLES OF LEARNING AND CHANGE

Unfortunately, counselors often assume that the client is resistant rather than considering the possibility of an inadequate approach. It is too simplistic to always attribute lack of progress in counseling to the client's resistance. Involuntary clients are not as likely as voluntary clients to adapt to the counselor's style. That is, an involuntary client who agrees to participate after some preliminary talking may not remain convinced that counseling is valuable if the counselor's approach does not seem sensible as the sessions progress. Imagine that a husband is talked into trying counseling by his wife. The man has a high school degree and operates heavy machinery for a living. The counselor begins by taking an extensive family history, including information about the couple's parents and grandparents. The wife enjoys the discussion, but the husband does not because he does not see how it relates to their problems. Regardless of how theoretically relevant the information is, a present-focused, action-oriented man who was reluctant to enter counseling in the first place will soon renew his reluctance and resist coming to counseling. It is important, then, to try to adapt to clients rather than stick religiously to an approach that will drive them away.

People learn in different ways. It is especially important to consider the learning style of the involuntary client, who may be less adaptable than the voluntary client. A brief listing of ways that people change should highlight some of the choices of approach that counselors can consider.

1. *Insight.* This is the basis for much counseling, but many people do not change behavior through better cognitive understanding, or they find that understanding hard to achieve. Other methods may be necessary to communicate a message.

2. *Modeling.* Some clients will learn best by seeing the appropriate behavior displayed. Counselors can demonstrate the behavior themselves or arrange a demonstration.

3. *Behavior rehearsal.* This is the "try it, you'll like it" technique. Clients may grudgingly agree to try on a new behavior, then discover they like it. Role-playing often follows a demonstration of the behavior and is followed by a real trial of the behavior. For example, a client who needs to learn how to express feelings may observe a counselor's self-disclosure, then practice self-disclosure in role-playing with the counselor before trying to talk openly with friends or family members.

4. *Self-esteem.* Some people improve markedly in all areas of functioning when they feel better about themselves. This enhancement of self-image is most often made possible by achievement and recognition, not direct discussion of self-worth.

5. *Relationships.* Some people improve when in the presence of an empathic counselor or friend who allows them to open up and be themselves without criticism or judgment.

6. *Group pressure.* The power of the emotional field of the group and family is awesome. Peer cultures may work better than individual therapy. Sometimes it is easier to help the client change by influencing the family first, and sometimes the identified client may not be able to respond to direct suggestions whereas family members can. Thus, the path of least resistance (and effort) may be through a slightly circuitous route.

7. *Reinforcement.* Much behavior is influenced by reaction to it in the environment. An unresponsive environment inadequately rewards behavior change. It is often difficult for counselors to affect the external environment, but sometimes this is possible. For example, a child having difficulty in school may be helped by having the teacher or principal arrange immediate feedback and praise for slight improvements in the child's behavior that previously may have been overlooked.

Many behaviorists ascribe all treatment failures to the therapist's inability to adequately understand what maintains the behavior. Thus, there is no such thing as client resistance, only therapist incompetence (Lazarus and Fay, 1982). Counselors need to assess in each client the most likely motivator for change, then tailor the treatment to the client.

8

Stages of Accessibility in Institutional Treatment

Chapter Eight

There are many models for institutional treatment: therapeutic communities, token economies, teaching parent homes, and positive peer cultures, to name a few. Each has its own strengths and weaknesses for such different client groups as the mentally ill, the delinquent or criminal, and the substance abusers. Some facilities choose a particular counseling theory, such as transactional analysis or reality therapy, and attempt to structure institutional policy and procedure around that theory, hoping for staff consistency and a unified approach.

It is important to remember that not all involuntary clients are alike. Some may have antisocial personalities that call for a strict system of accountability for behavior in the institutional context. Other involuntary clients may be rebellious and difficult to engage in counseling, but for emotional reasons. These are people who have the capacity to feel guilt and compassion for other people and would not be expected to intentionally inflict harm on others. Riche (1979) noted that she had worked with only two truly voluntary youths in her time as a social worker at the Children's Hospital at the Menninger Foundation. Though many of these children were diagnosed as having antisocial or borderline personalities, others were not. Yet all were coerced into treatment.

How the counselor views clients will depend to a great extent on his or her own personality and theories about why people behave as they do. For example, many drug abusers do have antisocial personalities, but others do not. Treatment must take these differences into account. Differential diagnosis is an ongoing problem, as there is little empirical evidence to demonstrate that borderline, narcissistic, and antisocial personalities can be differentially diagnosed (Harris and Kirk, 1985).

Unfortunately, the reality of institutional treatment is usually far different from theory. This disparity has important implications for working with involuntary clients who are often cynical about authority that seems not to practice what it preaches. But despite the gap between theory and practice, there are observable stages of institutional treatment through which the involuntary client passes. Understanding these stages will help the counselor respond appropriately to the clients at their level of development.

THEORY VS. REALITY IN INSTITUTIONAL TREATMENT

A common deterrent to implementing theories of treatment is that many counseling theories are not readily translated into institutional policy. The permissiveness of a client-centered model is fine inside the counselor's office but becomes problematic when administrators are trying to decide what to do about infractions of institutional rules. Some institutions establish token economies for ward or dormitory life, but counselors in sessions think in contradictory theoretical terms. For example, in the token economy/behavior modification model, it is not important to understand why a client broke a rule. Understanding inner mental events is considered as being of secondary importance to establishing a reliable connection between behavior and consequences in the environment through punishment and reinforcement. However, in most individual counseling models, the intent of the person is important to know in determining whether criticism or praise is suitable. Consequently, clients get one view of their behavior from the environment, still another from their counselor.

Many institutions and programs are based on a hospital or medical model in which a diagnosis is made and treatment prescribed. The assumption of pathology in the client encourages an aura of staff superiority and authority. Counselors who prefer more egalitarian approaches and who dislike labeling clients will have some adjustments to make in dealing with this model. Family systems counselors have an even greater problem because of their view that pathology does not reside in the person but in the system that produced the symptomatic behavior. These differences in theoretical approach affect client management and treatment recommendations as well as institutional climate.

An important consequence of some treatment models is the assignment of status and power within the institution. Democratically structured therapeutic communities are difficult to maintain because the highly educated staff are not given some of the satisfying perquisites of power. Custodial staff, in theory, do not act as mere functionaries but as respected and equal members of the team. In practice, however, many professionals work against a system that denies them direct control of treatment and activities in the program. Consequently, in a medical model environment a rift commonly develops between the professional and the custodial or security staffs. Doctors begin to see clients for their weekly or daily appointments while other staff feel left out of the therapeutic process, or worse, begin to question the doctor's judgment about a client whose day-to-day behavior he or she never observes. Goffman (1961) described the effects of a total institutional environment on the behavior of clients, staff, and professionals; yet these considerations are seldom incorporated into theories of counseling and treatment.

The rift between professionals and other staff becomes especially polarized when difficult clients are in treatment. Aggressive, manipulative, or suicidal clients create incredible stress for staff in a program, but it is the worker on the ward who must deal with crises as they occur. Other professionals are seldom present when an assault or suicide attempt occurs. In fact, professionals sometimes exercise their options not to be around in order to avoid the stress. Thus, a vicious cycle develops in which the greater the stress, the greater the rift between professional and line staff. And the greater the gap, the more likely it is that there will be hard feelings. Misunderstandings and an overall dilution of the goals of treatment result as treatment on the ward turns from administering therapy to rigid application of rules to maintain safety and security. This atmosphere lends itself to "splitting" phenomena in which clients form special bonds with particular workers to the detriment of their affiliation with other workers or professionals.

The presence of extremely difficult and resistant clients with conduct disorders in a program that usually focuses on schizophrenic patients disrupts the treatment of those clients whose behavior is less crisis provoking, though not less pathological. Institutional treatment, then, deviates from theoretical underpinnings when the model being used is inappropriate for all clients in the treatment. Many public institutions have little control over who is admitted for treatment and, consequently, their programs degenerate into a confused hodgepodge of services aimed primarily at keeping the lid on crises. Line staff in these programs burn out quickly and then often resort to harsh authoritarian stances with clients while professionals distance themselves from the futility of treatment (Gordon and Beresin, 1983; Johanson, 1983).

Another gap between the theory and practice of treatment in institutions occurs because clients often come and go quickly through the revolving door in the admissions office. Financial pressures in public institutions sometimes require quick discharges based not on clinical judgment but on administrative need. Clients are admitted, stablized on medication, then released. Legal pressures prevent programs from holding involuntary clients longer than a few days in the absence of hard data to prove the client's dangerousness to self or others.

In prisons the offender who has a firm release date faces different pressures than the mental patient whose release time will be determined by psychiatrists. Offenders' degree of motivation for treatment and their adaptation to it will depend on the length and rigidity of the sentence as well as their prior institutional treatment. The shock reaction to incarceration so often observed in the first offender is often replaced by the more jaded attitude of the repeat offender.

In an institution with quick turnover of clients, a therapeutic interaction among clients is difficult to achieve regardless of the reason for the turnover because relationships are tenuous and unstable. Nevertheless, there are identifiable stages for treatment of the delinquent, involuntary client. A counselor who understands these stages is better equipped to recognize the client's likelihood of responding well to various interventions and is better prepared to counter the clients' manipulations and regressive behavior.

A CORRECTIONAL MODEL

Korn and McKorkle (1959) offered a description of the treatment process at successive stages of accessibility in adaptive offenders, whose anxiety is relatively low and who believe they are basically well-adjusted in an inferior world. Although written over two decades ago, this description still offers an informative and pragmatic examination of resistance in institutional treatment. The description is not as applicable to mental hospitals as to correctional programs, with the exception of hospitals treating patients with personality disorders, such as antisocial personalities.

As Korn and McCorkle noted, the adaptive offender usually comes to treatment at the earliest stage of accessibility. The authors did not, however, make explicit another unfortunate truth: Relatively few clients advance to the final stages of treatment because of premature release or the ineffectiveness of actual treatment. Many programs, in fact, offer scant treatment and others are beset with internal organizational problems such as staff conflict. Consequently, the authors' description of treatment often does not match reality. Nevertheless, the stages of accessibility discussed below provide a glimpse of what the reluctant client will pass through, if treatment is successful.

Clients involuntarily committed to treatment for conduct or personality disorders enter treatment with preconceived notions of the program and therapists. The process of treatment essentially becomes a continuous battle of mutual definition. The client's goal is to gain control of the situation. Thus, stage 1 is a struggle for domination. It is important to emphasize that the stages of treatment presented below apply not to general psychiatric patients but to patients with delinquency or character disturbance.

1. *The struggle for control* (Can I dominate you?)
In this first stage, the client (delinquent) presents a thinly disguised appeal for help in an attempt to dupe the therapist. Many therapists do, in fact, make the mistake of accepting this appeal as a genuine plea for help. But the better therapist response is to avoid rushing to help and instead to calmly question the patient about his involvement in and contribution to his predicament.

Once clients realize they will be unable to manipulate the therapist, they will escalate to threats of violence or suicide; hostility that can usually be handled with questions about precisely what they plan to do and to whom. When this escalation fails to create confusion and turmoil, the client's only remaining response is to reevaluate the therapist, changing the definition from "sucker" to "son-of-a-bitch." Therapists who have too strong a need to be liked frequently overreact at this stage by either rejecting the client or giving in to demands.

2. *Overt rebellion* (Can anybody stop me?)
Having failed to control the therapist, the patient now embarks on a mission to challenge the therapeutic milieu; the ward. The importance of mature "custodial" staff is emphasized at this stage because the patient attempts to manipulate the rules of the unit to gain advantage. A ward or unit that is so rigid as to prevent such manipulation totally becomes repressive, and staff soon feel uneasy, as though they are dictators. Too loose an environment creates opportunity for manipulation without correction and learning. Staff frequently withdraw, feeling helpless to exert any control. The patient must be caught at violations for change to occur. The patient who begins by being devious must advance to open defiance in order to begin the next stage of heroic suffering.

3. *Heroic suffering* (You can't break me.)
The martyr gains gratification from an audience whom he or she attempts to turn into allies against the "repressive" treatment program. The only effective counter to this stage is to deny the patient an audience by segregation from other patients, but not staff if possible. The patient, however, must not be mistreated in any way since this fuels the definition of the treaters as oppressors. The therapeutic response to complaints is to respond by calm investigation and measured response. It then becomes difficult for the patient to sustain the intensity of heroic suffering.

4. *Despair* (Does anybody give a damn?)
The patient begins to feel despair and a growing sense of futility. However, there may also be efforts to engage the therapist and staff in discussions about the fairness of punishments administered for prior misbehavior. It is tempting to enter these discussions, but it shouldn't be done until there has been a thorough, extended examination of the patient's responsibility for his or

her situation. Frequently, the patient will profess miraculous insight and sudden, enthusiastic endorsement of new ways of living. Such should be met with quiet skepticism because no comprehensive change occurs without practice and implementation.

5. *The emergence of self-doubt* (What am I doing wrong?)

At this stage the patient will mix anger at authority with self-disgust. The therapist should avoid drawing generalized moral principles for the patient here since these frequently sound like "I told you so" or at best like platitudes. The presence of client self-doubt also often makes the therapist feel "home free," but setbacks and regressions are to be expected because the patient has not had the freedom to translate insight into behavior. Many therapists want to rush to console the patient to help him or her feel better, but this temptation must also be resisted. Patients must "stew in their own juice" for awhile.

6. *Testing* (Can I make it?)

The patient is now desegregated and given free access to mix socially with other patients. The therapist's job now is to help the patient discuss and resist pressures to return to old patterns of relating. Patient and therapist can engage in more reflective, philosophical dialogue than in the beginning of treatment. Examination of values and feelings can occur. Aftercare planning can be done. It would be unusual to reach this stage of treatment in less than one year, but unfortunately it is the kind of counseling most therapists want to do much quicker than is possible.

In summary, the stages of treatment for the delinquent progress from a struggle for control to eventual mutual exchange and therapeutic reciprocity. Inpatient psychiatric programs also treat involuntary clients, but the nature of patients' problems is quite different. Unfortunately what often occurs is that the psychiatric model is used inappropriately for the wrong type of problem.

A PSYCHODYNAMIC HOSPITAL MODEL

Takahashi (1983) outlined the basic structure and function of a psychodynamically oriented treatment team for a psychiatric hospital. This outline provides an interesting contrast to the foregoing model by Korn and McCorkle and will help counselors fathom the working assumptions behind each approach. Many psychiatric patients, like all correctional inmates, are required or coerced into treatment because they pose a danger to themselves or to others (Berman and Segel, 1982). Whether different models of treatment are required for these two types of institutions will be examined.

Takahashi outlined three stages of treatment and treatment styles that staff may employ and noted the stage of treatment at which each style is effective. The first style is the protective and receptive style. The staff member is warm, gentle, empathic, stable, and nurturing. The psychodynamic model assumes that the patients will need to progress through treatment stages that mirror or recreate stages of personality development. Consequently, the severely regressed patient needs a hospital environment which corresponds to the environment needed by an infant. Thus, in the first stage of treatment the patient needs an environment in which he or she can exist safely and securely. The patient then needs to progress to relationships in which trust develops, first with staff and then with other patients, much like a child would do in the first three years of life with parents and then playmates.

The second treatment stage is characterized by the neutral style in which the staff member begins to objectively help the patient learn about himself. This style is appropriate for the middle stages of treatment and corresponds to early childhood levels of development. The therapist serves as an authority figure and the client replays earlier patterns of behavior and projects them onto the therapeutic situation.

The final stage of treatment employs the realistic style of treatment. The staff member appropriately shares his or her own feelings and thoughts about the patient. This style is appropriate for the final stages of treatment and can be viewed as a more adult-to-adult than parent-to-child relationship, with give and take and candid feedback.

The models for the adaptive delinquent and psychiatric patient are different in style and underlying assumptions. The adaptive delinquent model does not try to replicate a family environment to stimulate development of personality. Rather, Korn and McCorkle suggested that staff start with "detached questioning." This approach seems to parallel Takahashi's description of the neutral style occurring in the second stage of treatment in the psychiatric unit.

The model for adaptive delinquents stresses that only after the counselor has endured and thwarted testing, manipulation, and hostility by the delinquent does an openness to information and feedback emerge. This would correlate with the realistic style and last stage in the psychodynamic model.

The comparison of models for the delinquent and psychiatric patient is important, because inappropriate use of the models results in treatment failure. Many counselors intuitively and intellectually believe that all troubled people at the very beginning of treatment will require acceptance into a safe, secure, and empathic environment before change will occur. However, staff in programs for delinquent youth who use the traditional psychiatric model often become pessimistic or even disillusioned about the rate of change in their clients, and they are frequently manipulated and "burned" by clients who use the counselors' empathy against them. Many psychiatric patients with narcissistic disorders (Harris and Kirk, 1985) likewise have personalities that may be better suited to the model presented by Korn and McCorkle.

The theory of personality held by the counselor will shape selection of treatment. Psychodynamically oriented therapists, for example, will tend to select the model that takes advantage of knowledge of psychosexual stages of development. It should also be re-emphasized, as Korn and McCorkle noted, that some offenders need treatment such as that outlined by the psychodynamic model.

The issue boils down to the fact that no one treatment approach fits all clients and that flexibility in treatment and in programs is needed. Not every involuntary client will need a model such as the one outlined for adaptive delinquents, but many will. Other involuntary clients will respond early and readily to empathy, especially around their feelings about being coerced into counseling. The counselor must size up the situation and client and make a decision about how to proceed effectively.

9

Typologies and Techniques

Chapter Nine

To work effectively with involuntary clients, counselors must have a pragmatic grasp of different types. The counselor who can quickly identify a client's "bag of tricks" may be more able to set up strategies for working with the client.

By providing recognizable profiles of patterns observed in practice, counselors can constructively meet the resistance of involuntary clients. It is important to remember that the same behavior in two clients may be motivated differently. Thus, the counselor may choose to respond to a personal criticism in one case with empathy and in another case with confrontation.

A checklist developed by Dr. Wallace Verburg for use with school-age children is one method of assessing the type of client one is working with. The counselor should obtain the views of the client and the opinions of two or three people who know the client (i.e., a parent, teacher, or a caseworker).

Use of the checklist is simple. Clients with behaviors in the left and middle column are considered emotionally as opposed to behaviorally troubled. Such clients respond to rapport and relationship-building approaches that emphasize increased awareness of feelings.

Clients with behavior in the right-hand column typically are thought of as conduct-disordered and respond best to cognitive or behavioral approaches that emphasize structure and consequences for actions. These conduct-disordered clients present three general patterns: the verbal attacker, the defender, and the fogger.

Please check items that seem to be most descriptive of the child's behavior.

☐ Inappropriate fears	☐ Accident prone	☐ Truancy, tardiness
☐ Fear of school	☐ Bites fingernails	☐ Destructive
☐ Seeks reassurance	☐ Sucks thumb	☐ Defiant
☐ Worries	☐ Enuresis, soiling	☐ Bully, cruel
☐ Cries easily	☐ Tics	☐ Belligerent, fights
☐ Overly conscientious	☐ Excessive fantasy	☐ Sullen
☐ Extreme shyness	☐ Stutters	☐ Resents correction
☐ Withdrawn	☐ Infantile speech	☐ Lies
☐ Preoccupied	☐ No speech	☐ Cheats
☐ Isolates self	☐ Physical ailments	☐ Tattles
☐ Wants to be first	(asthma, allergies,	☐ Angers easily
☐ Whines	stomachaches,	☐ Temper tantrums
☐ Rejected by peers	headaches)	
☐ Unhappy		
☐ Perfectionist		

THE VERBAL ATTACKER

The verbal attacker is the resistant client who believes in the adage "the best defense is a good offense." Most often attacking clients come from the following populations:

1. *Teenagers*

Certainly not all teenagers, but many of those who are referred to counseling against their wishes use attack as the primary method to deal with the therapist. This methodology seems quite natural as many of these young people have used the attack with most, if not all, adults in their lives. The counselor may choose to view this attack as transference and begin to confront, clarify, and interpret, or the response may be to deal with the attack more indirectly.

The attack history usually begins with verbal attacks on parents when teenagers either do not get what they want, or are told to do what they do not want to do. The parental request, "Please clean your room," is met with shouts like, "You're always on my back" or "Why are you always on my case?" When told they cannot stay out Saturday night until the early morning hours, these teens will angrily attack parents with, "You can't make me come in then," or "I should be able to do what I want." Escalation of conflict between teenagers and parents often ends in violence.

When teenagers are out of control, the school counselor, therapist, social worker, or psychologist is asked to intervene. But by this time the pattern is well established.

2. *Prison populations, group home residents*

These clients are often but not always teenagers. Differences between this population and the teenagers discussed above are their level of sophistication and the intensity of their attacking.

This population has become involved with the legal system. Hence, these clients are often much more daring in pushing limits than other teens. They will sometimes begin the relationship with the counselor with cursing and subsequent verbal abuse, ranging from putting down the counslor's professional competency to questioning the counselor's personal life.

In addition to being more daring, a high percentage of this population has a moderate to extensive background in receiving counseling services. This means that although clients may use the verbal attack as their primary ploy, they can convincingly change roles and give counselors what they want to hear.

3. *Substance abusers*

Again, this client is frequently a teenager and may be part of a corrections population. All that has been discussed above about the first two groups is salient here.

Adult abusers may be highly sophisticated. Their attack mode may appear only when pushed on either their involvement in counseling or on their drug/alcohol problems. With age and experience often come subtle and calculated maneuvers, more so than with volatile teens.

Common ploys of the attacker

Verbal attackers may use their favorite weapon at any time during the therapy process. They may use the verbal attack in any way possible, ranging from attempts to devalue the therapist's competence and ability to understand to random screaming. The put-down usually takes one of two forms. The first is the personal put-down. Some favorite issues of verbal attackers are:

1. The sex of the therapist. Rather than frontally attacking the sex of the therapist, the verbal attacker seems to enjoy putting the therapist in a bind, such as: (female client to male therapist) "You don't know what it is like to be a woman! You can't know the emotional conflicts a woman feels. What makes you think you can help me?"

2. The age of the therapist. This attack is the favorite among teenage verbal attackers. The dialogue, or monologue, begins: "You don't know what it's like for kids these days. You never had to go through what we have to go through. You're just like all the rest of the adults, a phony and a hypocrite. You can't help me, and if you were honest you would admit it."

3. The appearance of the therapist. Teenagers and prisoners seem to like this ploy. For example: "Man you are ugly. What are you staring at anyway?" Since most therapists like to maintain good eye contact, this strategy challenges the therapist's insecurities about his or her appearance and beliefs about effective interpersonal relationships.

4. The therapist's family life. This is perhaps the favorite of the personal put-downs. This can involve attacking the therapist's marital status ("You're divorced, and you're going to try to help me?") Or some teenagers will subtly inquire whether the therapist has children. If the answer is no, then this deficiency in experience can be used.

5. Denial of need. Many clients protest, "I don't need to be here." Like other ploys, this tactic has more than one form. The two most common scenarios seem to be (1) I don't need to be here and I never needed to be in counseling, or (2) I don't need to be in counseling anymore.

With the first form, the client will probably start the tactic during the initial session. With this maneuver, the client will usually be either "innocent" or sullen and defiant. "Innocent" clients will claim that this is " . . . all a mistake." Such clients will state that they don't know why or how they came to be in counseling. The innocent tactic has advantages. If there is no one to verify the reason(s) why the client is referred, the counselor is left with hearsay and must either confront or accept the client's statements. Doubting without confronting is difficult to do. The innocent tactic often evokes in the counselor a tendency to 'pity the poor person' or to become angry with the client. Either way the client is in control and is not getting the needed therapy.

The other common "I don't need to be here" tactic involves the client declaring that the therapy is over and that there is no need to come anymore. This tactic may follow the client saying, "Therapy has done me a world of good. I feel that I have improved and I don't need to be here." This tactic is often tempting for the counselor because it tends to validate the counselor's work.

6. Threats. Occasionally, therapists will encounter clients who attempt to dominate the therapy process by threatening the therapist. Usually clients who try this ploy are in the corrections system. However, teenagers who have been allowed to be out of control may also have learned to use threats to "get their way" and will attempt to intimidate the therapist. Likewise, substance abusers will infrequently make threatening statements, most often vague references to contacts they have who will hurt the therapist if he or she does what the client does not want done.

Threats may be direct or indirect. The direct threat from the person who has become part of the criminal justice system says, "I'm going to hurt you. I will either hurt you physically, or if it is not in my (the client's) best interest to hurt you physically, I will hurt you in another way." The other way may be to hurt the counselor's status with other clients. Teenagers who make threats will most likely threaten property.

The indirect threat resembles the vague direct threat in that it is meant to threaten in an unspecified manner. It is unlike the vague direct threat in that the client will not assert, "I will get you." Rather, the client will hint, "You know you could get hurt if you continue to press me on this issue," or "I had another counselor ask me that once and his car got sugar in the gas tank."

The obvious goal of the threat is to intimidate. The less glaring goal is to divert the counselor from therapeutic issues and send the counseling process down a dead-end road.

7. Combinations. The sophisticated attacker is able to use the above six ploys in combinations. Like the boxer who is able to coordinate punches in a flurry to destroy the enemy, the sophisticated attacker is able to use the above tactics in effective combinations to divert and dominate the counselor.

For instance, the attacker may use a put-down, followed by an "I don't need to be here," followed by aggressive silence: "You know, you are too old to relate to me. You don't know what it is like to have the pressures teenagers have nowadays. Besides, your parents were probably never divorced. I really don't need to be here. You and everyone else are always hassling me. Why don't you get off my case? Fine, you can make me come here, but you can't make me talk."

This combination gives the therapist plenty of chances not only to be dominated but to be diverted from counseling. The put-down ("You are too old to relate to me. You don't know what it is like to have pressures teenagers have nowadays. Besides your parents were probably never divorced . . .") can easily divert therapists into a scenario of trying to prove they are not too old and that they can relate to teens and their pressures. Further, therapists whose parents were divorced can tell the client that they come from a divorced family. In that case, the attacker could follow with another combination with full knowledge that the therapist fell for the first attack. If therapists do not come from a divorced family, and if they answer this line of attacking, they are left with trying to prove that they can relate to someone who has divorced parents.

The put-down was followed by an "I don't need to be here" statement ("I really don't have to be here. You and everyone else are always hassling me. Why don't you get off my case?") If counselors try to answer these allegations, they will be sucked into justifying their existence in the session. In answering this aspect of the attacker's combination, counselors are setting themselves up for being dominated or diverted.

The final part of this combination is the aggressive silence (" . . . you can make me come here, but you can't make me talk.") As stated earlier, aggressive silence reaps many dividends for the attacker who immobilizes the counselor, controls the session, maintains secrecy, and cuts off the therapeutic process.

Whether this one, or any of the many combinations that can be used by the sophisticated attacker, the importance for the therapist is as follows: Remember that the combination is made up of the above discussed ploys; it is nothing new. It can be broken down into its respective parts. When the combination is broken down into a process of different ploys, the therapist can identify the combination, not become overwhelmed by it, and deal with the combination in an effective manner. As suggested by Korn and McCorkle (1959), the primary task at the beginning of work with these clients is to avoid being manipulated and to enter into detached questioning.

In the beginning of work with many involuntary clients, detached questioning is aimed at getting specific detailed information about the facts of the client's life as the client knows them. Then the counselor attempts to get clarification about how the client interprets, explains, incorporates, and deals with these facts but without challenging these thoughts, beliefs, and feelings. The counselor seeks clarification by pointing out what he or she observes about the client, especially patterns of behavior, e.g.; "You always frown when we start talking about your attending Alcoholics Anonymous meetings."

The counselor may also need to deal with in-session behavior by pointing out attempts to divert, threaten, or confuse the counselor, but the counselor usually avoids asking for an explanation of these behaviors early in counseling. Yochelson and Samenow (1978), however, recommended that the counselor relate these behaviors to thinking patterns, such as the desire and plan to control and dominate others.

The counselor will eventually confront clients with statements about contradictory thoughts or behavior ("You say you want to be a responsible parent, but you never pay any child support to your ex-wife.") Ultimately, most counselors try to help the client reach a level of self-understanding through development of insight. Many clients never achieve this level of counseling, and a more practical goal is to be able to help clients weigh the plusses and minuses of a variety of options open to them. Even this level of counseling, however, requires that the counselor not be sidetracked by the tactics of the client. Whatever counseling approach is taken must be based on recognition of the tactics of the client.

Hartman (1978), on the other hand, recommended an essentially client-centered approach. He said that the client feels that he or she cannot be understood and therefore what is needed is a more empathic response. Hartman recommended that counselors put themselves in the client's place and not take anger or other attacks personally. He recommended having faith in the client as a person and not passing judgment. All these recommendations are fine for the person who is involuntary but essentially emotionally maladjusted.

Yochelson and Samenow (1977) provided a rather stark assessment of the tactics of people with highly irresponsible behavior (criminals) and they recommended confronting these persons by pointing out what tactics they use to regain the maximum advantage in the interview. These tactics are:

1. Building themselves up while putting the examiner down. The examiner is seen as someone to overcome. The criminal tries to put others down to avoid a put-down him or herself.
2. Feeding the examiner what the criminal thinks he or she wants to hear. The criminal tries to convince the examiner that he or she is sincere and has good intentions.
3. Feeding the examiner what the criminal thinks he or she ought to know. He only tells what puts him or herself (criminal) in a good light.
4. Lying. Criminals know the truth will work against their interests. Lies of omission are most common.
5. Vagueness. He or she does this to avoid being put on the spot.
6. Attempting to confuse. If this occurs, the criminal feels he or she has gained the upper hand. They can use this confusion later if questioned about a discrepancy.
7. Minimization. If a violation occurs and the criminal is caught, he or she will make his or her actions look as though they were no big deal.
8. Diversion. The criminal will talk about irrelevant material to divert the examiner to something less important.
9. Assent. The criminal will falsely agree with the examiner to abbreviate discussion, and by agreeing he or she will not alienate the examiner.
10. Silence. This is done to maintain secrecy, and is also an extremely potent form of control.

Some of the tactics used by the criminal during the change process are:

1. Selective attention and perception. He or she will only pay attention to things that conform to his or her objectives.
2. Total inattention. The criminal's mind wanders miles away.
3. Tardiness and missing appointments. He or she offers phony excuses.
4. Feeding the agent of change what the criminal thinks he or she wants to hear by
   a. Confession. Merely a tactic to score points.
   b. Showing insight. The agent will hopefully ignore the violation and be pleased with the insight.
   c. Specializing in leadership. Tries to falsely demonstrate he or she is changing.
   d. Tailoring the approach. He or she tries to structure his or her presentation toward the personality and views of the agent.

5. Misunderstanding. If the criminal fails to perform, he or she states there was a misunderstanding between him or her and the agent.
6. Generalizing a point to absurdity. The criminal will take a point to an absurd extreme.
7. Deliberate postponement. When the criminal has little intention of doing something, he or she will postpone it.
8. Claiming that he or she has changed enough to leave the program.
9. Putting the agent of change on the defensive through tactics of the attack. He or she tries to usurp the role of teacher and to convert others to his or her point of view.

Generally, the attacker is a teenager, substance abuser, or someone involved in the criminal justice system. This is not to imply that a majority or even a large percentage of teenagers, substance abusers, or criminal justice clients are attackers, but the greatest number of attackers seem to come from these groups.

The attacker has a repertoire of common ploys that he or she uses. Their common goal is (1) to dominate the counselor and the counseling process, and/or (2) to divert the counseling from therapeutic issues.

THE DEFENDER

Defenders do not believe that they can dominate the counseling process by direct attack, so this type of client tries to control the counseling by covert methods meant (1) to let the counselor believe that there is progress being made, and/or (2) to lull the counselor into a nice comfortable, counseling process in which there will be no confrontation.

Aside from the obvious differences between the attacker and the defender, there are some subtle differences and similarities that need to be noted. In contrast to the attacker, who does not want to be in counseling, defenders often are ambivalent about coming to counseling. They are confused about whether they really want to fully engage in counseling or want to change. Many are spouses or children who come to counseling wanting to please a husband, wife, or parent.

In contrast to the attacker, who has often been coerced into coming to counseling, defenders come because they want to secure the approval of a family member or another important person in their lives, and so are coerced in a different sense because they are seeking something (but not change) rather than avoiding consequences. Batterers are a good example of this because they come to counseling often to convince their wives they are changing so they can all get back together as a family.

Common ploys of the defender

Unlike the attacker, who uses the attack obviously and directly, defenders intertwine their ploys throughout the counseling process and, if they are adroit at their methods, the counselor will not know what is happening. In fact, the counselor may even believe that the counseling is going well. Common ploys of the defender are:

1. Giving the counselor what the counselor wants to hear. This is the method behind all the devices of the defender. Sometimes the defender is quite aware of what he or she is doing, but sometimes not. When the tactic is conscious, there is a greater chance that the client is antisocial or criminal. In carrying out this ploy, defenders may begin by trying to impress the counselor with sincerity and/or let the counselor know that they are confused about the nature of counseling. Both the sincerity and confusion have immediate payoffs for defenders; diversion, and a chance for the client to size up the therapist. By getting the counselor to respond sincerely to the clients sincerity/confusion the client gets an initial impression about what the therapist wants to hear. For instance, the scenario may begin:

Client: (in a concerned, meaningful tone of voice) I am glad I'm here in counseling, but I just don't know how to begin. I don't know what to talk about.
Counselor: Well, why don't you talk about whatever is on your mind.

In this case, the counselor has just opened the flood gates for the client to talk about anything from last night's television schedule to the Middle East. After a period of time, when the counselor confronts this with a "Why don't we get down to business?" defenders can retort that they are only doing what the counselor asked. Or the client can follow the directive to get down to business by using the ploys discussed below.

2. Selective attention. This is the tactic of "hearing only what you want to hear." This tactic works for the defender extremely well because it uses nothing confrontive. The defender can quietly "listen" to the counselor, seemingly agree with everything the counselor is saying, then leave the session. The problem is that the clients leave the session hearing only those things with which they agree, ignoring all else.

For example, a session may touch upon the issue of a husband not showing attention to his wife. During the session, the therapist may believe that, although the husband gives little attention, he does love his wife. Through selective attention the defender will remember that the counselor said that the husband loves his wife and ignore all other material about the session.

Counselors are often taught to check the client's understanding of what the counselor has said. Checking out understanding is a good practice, but the defender who is skilled at selective attention will use it repetitively.

Counselor: Please tell me your understanding of what I have just said about your not giving attention to your wife.
Husband: You said that I love my wife.
Counselor: That is only a part of the message. The main thing I want you to understand is that you often don't give your wife much attention. What is your understanding about what I have said of your relationship with your wife.
Husband: I understand that part of what you have said is that I love my wife.

These exchanges can be highly frustrating for a therapist, especially when the client carries selective understanding ad infinitum. When carried out in a "sincere" manner by the client, many therapists find this tactic very difficult to confront. Of course, when not confronted, the defender can keep the counseling process in an ineffective loop.

3. Confessing. The act of confessing has long been associated with constructive change. In some religions, as well as some psychological theories, confession is regarded as a prerequisite for change. In counseling, confessing can be very constructive and may be needed for some clients. There are, however, clients who use confession as a tactic to avoid constructive change.

For purposes of detecting confessing, it will be helpful to divide confessors into two groups: the straight confessor and the partial confessor.

Straight confessing is confessing to impress, such as, "I did it, what I did was awful. I feel terribly guilty. I'm so sorry." Although this is the basic scenario, the straight confession ploy itself may be drawn out over fifteen to thirty minutes or more.

An offshoot of the straight confession is the partial confession. In using this ploy, the client will discuss and dwell upon only certain aspects of any problem. Hence, in the partial confession the client admits to any number of minor problems or infractions and by such admissions uses the sessions to divert the counselor into making "progress" in areas that amount to no substantial change. Client payoffs of the partial confession include avoiding major problem areas, diverting the counseling process, and controlling the process in an indirect, covert manner.

In contrast to the attacker, the defender using confession does not like or want to be confronted. Confrontation sometimes forces the defender into different defense patterns. The sophisticated defender who is deft at employing the straight confession can slide from confessing about a problem area into confession about his confessing:

Counselor: (confronting the client) Joe, I have heard you telling me how badly you feel about fighting in the school halls. You have told me of your guilt and terrible feelings several times before. Frankly, I believe you are using your confessing to me to avoid some real issues.

Client: Mr. Jones, you are right. I have been trying to put you on . . . I'm sorry. I do a lot of that. I'm really sorry for doing that.

At this point the counselor is likely to take the bait and not confront the client about using confession to avoid responsible change. Confession is not confronted or in another way constructively handled. The counseling process is bogged down with continuing confessions, and the client is again rewarded for playing the confession game.

A final twist on the confession tactic that the defender may employ can be termed the false confession. The false confession is simply admitting to actions that the client did not commit. For example, a student may admit to talking in class when in fact he did not talk at all. An inmate may admit to stealing commissary items. There are payoffs that the client obtains from the false confession. First, this ploy can confuse the counselor.

When the counselor expects overt resistance and is then hit with a confession, there is a tendency to deal with the area which has been "confessed." Second, the false confession puts the client in control of the counseling process.

Whether the defender is using one, two, or three forms of confession, the counselor needs first to ascertain if the client is using the confession as a tactic to avoid change. The counselor then needs to identify the type(s) of confessing being used. Since these tactics boil down to issues of control, the counselor needs to confront the client with this in mind and try to help the client see how the behavior generalizes into other areas of life.

4. Insight (sudden or otherwise). As with confession, some psychological theorists put great importance on the client being able to show insight. Other schools of psychology deny any importance of insight. The point of interest here is when the client is using "insight" as a method of resistance.

The client who makes use of insight as a means of resistance often is a young, verbal, affluent, successful person. This client is usually well read in psychology and often has had previous counseling. This is not to say that other types of clients do not use insight as a means to avoid change. Students are sometimes surprisingly adroit at using psychological terms and showing insight. Clients from correctional systems will sometimes use insight, especially those corrections clients who have been exposed to repeated counseling.

There are two major indicators that insight is being used for the purpose of resisting. The first is the use of psychological jargon. The second is the unwillingness of clients to act upon any of their "insights."

In looking for the use of psychological jargon as an indicator of "insight" as a resistance, repetition is the key word. When the counselor begins to hear "... suppress my anger ..." or "... Freudian slip ..." or "... my dream analysis ..." or other terms repeatedly, one may be listening to a person who is using "insight" to resist the therapy process.

An even better indicator of using "insight" is client failure to carry out assignments. The sophisticated client will have many plausible reasons for not completing (or even starting) assignments. The counselor should be careful to ensure that assignments are achievable and have not been forced upon the client.

5. Misunderstanding. A client can use misunderstanding basically in two ways. The first is to misunderstand about what was said in the session. The second is to misunderstand during the session.

Misunderstanding about the session is a ploy to allow defenders to extricate themselves from unpleasant assignments between sessions. For example, a father who agreed on an assignment to talk with his teenage son about their relationship may return to the next session saying that he didn't exactly know what he was supposed to talk about with his son. This may be a legitimate reason for the father not to talk with the son about their relationship. The next session, the father again reports that he didn't really understand and would like to go over the explanation again. At this point, the counselor may begin to sense (or resense) the father's reluctance to talk with the son. If, in fact, the father is reluctant, another explanation of the assignment will probably prove fruitless. The father is using misunderstanding as a tactic to get out of talking with his son.

The other manner in which misunderstanding can be used by the defender is to "misunderstand" during the session. This differs from misunderstanding about the session in that the client is not interacting about what happened last session or between sessions, he is misunderstanding right now, during the session. As an example, the same counselor and father are in a session:

Counselor: Joe, it appears that you have virtually no relationship at all with your son. You tell me that you have not said anything except 'hello' to him for the past year; that when he is at home he spends virtually all of his time in his room; that you are suspicious of what he is doing up in his room. You tell me that he is gone most of the time, and when he is home he usually doesn't even see you, talk with you, or even eat dinner with you. You seem to have no relationship with him.

Father: I don't know what you mean about us not having a relationship.

At this point more explanation about the counselor's view of the relationship will probably do no good. The father is probably using misunderstanding to covertly control the session.

Misunderstanding can be used on virtually any subject about and/or during the counseling. There are, however, some subjects that this type of defender seems to favor. These areas include:

a. Being late for appointments. "Gee, I thought that the appointment was for four-thirty, not for four o'clock." A twist on the misunderstanding of appointment times is the client being early for an appointment. "Gee, I came in at three-fifteen for the three-thirty appointment and waited a half hour until three forty-five. I thought the appointment was for three-thirty, not four o'clock."

b. Not carrying out assignments or not doing what was agreed upon to perform an assignment. "Gee, I thought you meant to take my son out for ice cream, not to talk with him about a serious subject."

c. Missing appointments due to "misunderstanding." "Gee, I thought the appointment was for today, Friday. I didn't know you had it down for Thursday."

A final misunderstanding is not usually used by defenders unless they see that their "back is up against the wall" and feel highly defensive. This final type of misunderstanding is usually employed by the attacker and could be categorized perhaps under professional put-downs or misunderstandings. The response from the client to the counselor is, "You don't understand me." As noted earlier, some teenage clients and some clients in the corrections system seem to rely upon this type of response.

"Misunderstanding" can either be a client genuinely struggling to ascertain aspects of the counseling process or a ploy to lead the counselor down a dead-end street.

6. Socializing. Many socializing defenders are young, achieving, verbal, intelligent, and social. It is natural that when these clients feel uncomfortable or forced into the counseling process, they will fall back upon

behaviors with which they feel comfortable. One of those behaviors is to socialize.

The easiest socializer for the counselor to detect is the blatant socializer. This is the client who wants to talk about the weather, the President, baseball, the economy, etc. Most counselors, even beginning counselors, are able to detect this type of defender. Socializing is not the same as gaining rapport with the client. The counselor who allows socializing to occur under the guise of building rapport is misguided and wasting time.

Some defenders socialize by attempting to manipulate counselors into talking about themselves. The counselor may fall for this ploy if he or she defines talking about himself or herself as "self-disclosure." To be effective, self-disclosure must be in the client's best interest, brief, and infrequent.

A spinoff of the above is the client who is in counseling for marriage/family therapy and is able to keep the focus of counseling on his or her spouse and/or children. In marriage/family therapy this is a highly effective ploy as counselors are often reluctant to refocus clients whenever the content of the session concerns therapeutic matters.

THE FOGGER

Foggers are a combination of the attacker and the defender. They have the attitude of the attacker and use the methodology of the defender. Foggers may be adults, adolescents, or children. They may be middle-class, wealthy, or materially poor. This type of client may be from a criminal setting or have had no criminal involvement whatsoever.

Common ploys of the fogger

1. *Lying by omission.* The fogger will "forget" to mention salient facts or issues important to the therapy process. For instance, a family has been referred because the father has tried to sexually abuse his teenage daughter. In relating the incident, the father, using the attacker's philosophy of being on the offensive and the defender's methodology of using covert behaviors meant to lull the counselor into thinking the therapy process is going well, lies by omission by telling the counselor only what he (the father) believes the counselor already knows.

Father: I tried to sexually abuse my daughter.
Counselor: Can you tell me the specifics of what happened?
Father: I was lying on the bed and she walked into my bedroom.
Counselor: Tell me more.
Father: Well, she tried to come into my bedroom while I was on the bed.
Counselor: Yes, I understand that. What happened that caused her to come into your bedroom?
Father: I said something.
Counselor: What did you say?
Father: I called her name.
Counselor: Did you say anything else?
Father: Yes.

Counselor: What else did you say?
Father: I said, "Joanne, come into the bedroom."

In this interaction, the father has never blatantly told a lie. He has not denied anything about the incident. He has, however, each step of the way lied by deliberately leaving out important aspects of the incident.

In addition to the above tactic of telling the counselor what the counselor knows and then simply answering with minimal (though not untruthful) information, the fogger will use the phrase, "I can't exactly remember," or "I don't exactly know." These phrases should not be confused with the attacker's outright "I don't know." The fogger uses the "I don't exactly know" as a means of lying by omission, and is amenable to a less confrontational approach than needed with the attacker.

2. *Being vague.* The ability (or disability) to be less than clear is the first cousin of the lie by omission. The difference is one of degree. When lying by omission, the fogger gives the counselor nothing except what is directly ascertained. When the fogger is being vague, the counselor is given a small amount of information. In the example of the incestuous father who called his daughter into the bedroom, his being vague rather than lying by omission may have led to the following dialogue:

Father: Well, I wanted her to come into the bedroom and something was said.
Counselor: What was said?
Father: Well, there was something said along the lines of her coming into the bedroom.
Counselor: Who said what?
Father: Well, there were some words about her coming into the bedroom.
Counselor: Who said the words and what was said?
Father: Well, I guess that I said it in words and she kind of said it with her being seductive before.

The father has succeeded in being vague. Although the counselor has made some progress in getting the father to be more specific about the incident, the father's final remark reopened the flood gates of vagueness. How was the daughter being seductive, if, in fact, she was being seductive? What does the word "before" mean? That evening? That day? A week before the incident? As with the other types of resisters, foggers will drop back to their favorite ploys and the counselor must stay aware of repeat performances of the tactics.

3. *Minimizing.* With this ploy, the fogger attempts to control and confuse the process by minimizing the harm of problem behaviors. Common phrases to be aware of that show when the fogger is minimizing are: "It's not that big a deal," "You're making a mountain out of a molehill," and "What I did was nothing compared to what so-and-so did." Continuing with the example of the father:

Father: What I did sexually was a one-time thing which was caused by my reading sex magazines. I never did anything like that before and I'm sure that I'll never do it again.

The counselor, in order to deal with this minimizing, must be able to escape the trap of the reductionist argument by pointing out the harm that has been done by the client's behavior. The temptation is great to let clients off the hook by allowing them to minimize the significance of their acts, but counselors must not be afraid to take a stand and outline clearly the consequences of the client's behavior.

Intervention with attackers, defenders, and foggers can be planned from a variety of perspectives. The counselor must first be aware of what is occurring behaviorally and then must relate those behaviors to some theory of human behavior. Korn and McCorkle (1959), as reviewed earlier, stated that the counselor's responses must be geared to the accessibility of the client to counseling. The general rule of thumb is to avoid attempts to manipulate, stay calm, ignore as much of the baiting as possible, and begin detached questioning. Empathy for the client's feelings about being coerced into counseling is appropriate, but the counselor must determine whether the client resents being coerced into counseling or more generally resents expectations that he or she behave responsibly.

10

Special Issues

Chapter Ten

Counselors who work with involuntary clients frequently must make difficult decisions about them. These decisions are often emotionally charged for several reasons:

1. The consequences of decisions for the client are serious. For example, decisions may affect whether the client will be incarcerated.
2. Clients' problems are serious enough that decisions about addressing the problems make counselors anxious about the effects of mistakes.
3. Involuntary clients may be sufficiently angry to threaten or to become violent. Decisions about how to react to violence or the threat of it are emotional because counselors must consider their own welfare.
4. The values of clients may be repugnant to counselors.
5. Counselors are often caught in a web of conflicting pressures and loyalties because they represent and answer to their employer, yet their training teaches them to be loyal to their clients. Sometimes the interests of employers and the wishes of clients may clash. For example, when damaging information is disclosed in sessions, how does the counselor decide whether to report that information?

The emotional intensity of the counseling process with involuntary clients increases the chances of errors in judgment. Mistakes occur when counselors have not clarified prior to confronting a problem their own values and ethical positions, and have not learned how to reduce their emotional reactiveness. Consequently, they often fail to think through a situation before acting. Also, counselors want to think the best about their clients and may be caught off guard and compromised through the client's manipulations.

In order to reduce therapeutic errors with involuntary clients, counselors need to understand their motives for being in the kind of work they are in, reflect on the ethical dilemmas inherent in working with involuntary clients, and anticipate common problems in order to be prepared for them. Counselors also need to understand not just the therapeutic relationship, but how emotional dynamics in groups and organizations can create pressure that leads to unwise decisions. And special clients can create special problems.

SELF-AWARENESS ISSUES

It is essential to examine the motivations of those who enter into this kind of work and why they stay. Counselors' actions toward their clients may be affected by their reasons for doing the work.

It is perhaps too simplistic to say that one's choice of work is a reflection of unresolved personal issues, but there is merit in that assertion. Counselors who themselves chafe at the imposition of authority may be trying to resolve their own problems with authority figures by working with others who have similar problems. Sometimes counselors, unable to rebel themselves, seem to get vicarious satisfaction from watching their clients act out. On the other hand, there are often practical reasons why people work in corrections or related fields, such as the availability of jobs.

Although motivation for major choices is always complex, it is enlightening to simplify, so let us categorize the primary motivations of counselors into three groups. First, there is the "save the cat on the roof" motivation. Many counselors enter their work hoping to rescue clients, a desire that may be genuinely altruistic. This desire also may derive from their own sense of having needed help at some point in their lives. People who have been helped often want to pass the favor on to others; people who have been neglected often want to do for others what was never done for them, much as parents want to give to their child a chance for travel or education that they never received. In moderation, the wish to rescue can be good, but the counselor driven by this motivation often gets stuck on the roof while the cat leaps to safety.

A second primary motivation for counselors is the "There but for the grace of God, go I" feeling. When working with clients who are in tragic circumstances, it is often apparent how easily our own lives could have taken a wrong turn without opportunities for education or the support of a loving family. Most counselors feel a moral obligation to help others less fortunate. Yet sometimes counselors may unconsciously feel that by helping another person they ward off tragedy for themselves. We all engage in this kind of thinking at times. We may give blood with the unconscious hope that the act will prevent misfortune from befalling us.

Again, in moderation, this is an appropriate motivation, but it is also essential to recognize that personal choices, those choices within a person's control, are responsible for most of the dilemmas clients bring into counseling. It is fine to empathize with the suffering of clients with problems but it is also important to believe that they could choose to be different than they are. Therefore, a hearty dose of the "There but for the grace of God, go I" feeling may cause the counselor to overlook the element of personal responsibility in people's predicaments. Counselors sometimes feel sorry for their clients, and thus let their clients "off the hook" inappropriately.

Finally, a motivation that brings some counselors to work with involuntary clients is the "stop crowding into line" reaction. When working with irresponsible people who have done something wrong, been caught, and forced into treatment, counselors sometimes want to participate in stopping them from doing it anymore, and they especially do not want their clients to get away with their misdeeds. This is the reaction we all experience when we are in a long line and someone crowds in front of us. The indignation makes us want to call the police or some other person in authority. This attitude must be monitored closely to prevent the counselor from becoming the enforcer of the moral code because few clients will respond positively to sermonettes.

PROBLEMS OF ALLIANCES IN INSTITUTIONS

Many therapeutic and ethical errors occur because counselors do not understand the dynamics of alliances in the institutional climate.

Clients in institutions frequently try to form a special alliance with one staff member, then attempt to use that alliance to pit staff members against each other. If successful, the consequence of this "splitting" is a divided, ineffective staff. Some clients are quite conscious of their manipulations; others maneuver without awareness, such as they did when they were children setting mother against father or parents against teacher in order to defuse the combined power of adults to control the child's behavior. Yet if counselors are to be effective in any setting, they must learn to recognize overinvolvement and inappropriate identification with clients.

Splitting usually is initiated when a client finds a weak or sympathetic spot in a staff member. For example, counselors may learn that a new client was a high school classmate or the friend of a friend. Or counselors with a new baby in the family discover that a client also has a new baby he has never seen. These discoveries create a special bond between counselor and client, and such bonds may make counselors especially protective and forgiving or more likely to listen to and believe criticism of another staff member. Sometimes counselors later learn that they were victims of inventions intended to play on their sympathies. Also, sometimes the formulation of the special relationship springs from a genuine camaraderie but is later used by the client to manipulate the counselor.

Splitting is accomplished when the counselor's judgment about a third person is distorted by special feelings for a client. A counselor may pay particular attention to a complaint about another staff member when the complaint is made by a favorite client. This favoritism does not have to occur only in the institutional setting. Private counselors often begin to take sides with their clients against courts or the court's representatives in services such as parole or probation. Clients might gripe that their parole officers are harrassing them and implore the counselor to ask the officer to stop. A parolee may present several instances of the alleged harrassment that sound very convincing. Should counselors angrily confront the officers with this information, their ability to communicate about their common client will be impaired.

In institutional settings, rifts often develop between treatment and custodial staffs as clients decry the callousness of one to the other. This is a common pattern of splitting in which one staff member, often treatment-oriented, takes on the role of protector while the other, the custodial or security person, becomes the disciplinarian — much like the hard and soft roles that fathers and mothers assume when they disagree about how to discipline their children.

Clients also may try to pit different shifts against each other by complaining to the people on their "favorite" shift about the lazy or cruel behavior of people on another shift. Frequently, the shift that works late night hours takes a relaxed approach to rules and regulations, perhaps because people associate night with relaxation and days with business. The differences in style between one shift and another provide opportunity for complaints about unnecessarily rigid staff. Also, workers in institutions, like people everywhere, need to feel appreciated and special. Unfortunately, this need often makes them vulnerable to manipulation.

Splitting has been studied under different names. In transactional analysis theory, three different roles constitute the three points on a triangle: victim, rescuer, and persecutor. Clients accomplish splitting by portraying themselves as victims in order to engage the rescuers sympathies and provoke action against persecutors.

Social psychologists explain this three-way interaction through cognitive dissonance theory in which these rules of human relationship apply: A friend of my friend is my friend, and an enemy of my friend is my enemy. Thus, the counselor who is "friends" with a client will be an enemy toward an enemy (the parole officer) of the client. Splitting occurs when the client forms a special bond with someone who becomes a friend, then turns that friend against another person who becomes an enemy to both.

In Bowen family therapy (Bowen, 1978), the process of splitting is discussed through the concept of triangulation. Triangulation means to have one's opinion of another person influenced by the opinions (gossip) of a third person rather than through direct personal contact and experience. For example, the counselor becomes angry at a parole officer because of a client's complaint. When the conversation between counselor and client consistently revolves around the officer, then the counselor is triangulated and productive change is blocked because the client is not dealing directly with his problems.

There will be times when counselors will need to side with their clients against unethical or unfair treatment by others. More often, however, counselors will need to avoid being manipulated into inappropriate and destructive behavior. Here are some suggestions for avoiding splitting.

1. *Awareness is crucial.*

Knowledge of the principles and typical examples of splitting help counselors to recognize what is occurring. But it is also important for counselors to have self-awareness about their own vulnerabilities. Counselors who harbor deep personal feelings about the unfairness of racial discrimination are perhaps more likely to sympathize with clients who complain that another staff member is bigoted.

Effective counselors develop an intuitive sense that they are being triangulated, compromised, manipulated, or split. One counselor described it as feeling as though he were trying to dig himself out of a deep hole being filled with sand. It is important to be able to recognize the funny or uneasy feeling that signifies trouble.

2. *Clear understanding of rules and boundaries is essential.*

Counselors must know precisely institutional rules and regulations to avoid bending the rules for a client. If the rules forbid contact with clients after their release, then this rule should be followed. A counselor may believe that he or she is being kind to offer a teenage boy a place to stay after his release from a youth center. But such an offer in most circumstances is at best inappropriate and may be grounds for dismissal. Counselors who do not understand the reasons for particular rules should ask supervisors about the reasons.

Ethical standards developed by professional groups such as social workers, counselors, and psychologists also define boundaries, such as the prohibition of sexual contact between counselor and client. These standards can seldom, however, do more than enunciate abstract principles, so counselors must constantly ask themselves whether it is appropriate to do such things as give rides, accept gifts, lend money, or agree to do other favors for clients.

If a counselor is in doubt, a supervisor should be consulted. When the relationship between the counselor and client is appropriate and professional, slips of judgment by third parties are rare. The counselor should not form an opinion about someone else without facts and personal knowledge, which enable good judgment to prevail.

3. *Counselors need to consider whether the problems are theirs or their clients.'*

Though counselors must, of course, empathize, they need not rescue the client from every situation. The client who complains about a parole officer may want the counselor to take sides, but the counselor should be wary about doing so. The counselor must find a way of being a "friend" to the client without becoming an enemy of the client's enemy. This is difficult to do because, as noted, people generally regard an enemy of a friend as an enemy. But mature people learn to escape the confinement of that rule, and counselors must also learn to define friendship with a client in terms of professional boundaries, limitations, and requirements that are different from ordinary friendships. In other words, counselors must define explicitly how counseling is different from friendship.

There are several particularly troublesome kinds of people who confront counselors working with involuntary clients: physically aggressive clients, substance abusers, and antisocial personalities. Counselors frequently make mistakes in judgment when working with these clients or question themselves, doubting they have done the right thing.

DEALING WITH PHYSICALLY AGGRESSIVE CLIENTS

In institutions and in private practice, male or female clients will occasionally threaten and/or actually assault the counselor. These threats and assaults can happen for many reasons, many having little to do with the person attacked. Inmates can become violent after receiving bad news in mail, visitation, or court appearances. One private practitioner was attacked for keeping a patient waiting who didn't have an appointment. The probability of violence increases with the client's degree of involuntariness, when the client perceives no alternatives.

Residential living staff members are more likely than most counselors to encounter violence from clients, if for no other reason than the vast amount of time spent with clients in the grind and stress of day-to-day life. These staff members do function as counselors, albeit sometimes informally, and need to be prepared for the occasional problem that arises. Not only is it difficult for counselors to be effective when they feel afraid or intimidated, the chances of serious flaws in judgment increase, making it all the more important to prepare for these situations.

Counselors should never assume they can reliably predict which clients are dangerous. They should, nevertheless, try to assess the existence or degree of dangerousness and take sensible precautions. There is a moral obligation to provide warning to the intended victim and to the police if a client threatens someone. The policies of some institutions prohibit serving clients who have made direct threats against staff members. Specific threats are more serious than ambiguous, general threats, but the rule of thumb is to err on the side of caution.

Many, perhaps most counselors feel uneasy or afraid in the face of anger and respond by either bluffing their way through or withdrawing from counseling. It is difficult to respond directly to another person's anger by calmly pointing out the behavior and how it represents a response to feelings of impotence and an attempt to control and manipulate. Women in our culture are especially susceptible to being intimidated through anger. Fear of a client paralyzes and inhibits effective counseling, but there are some things that can be done to bring the problem into the open to see if it can be managed.

Intimidation is often indirect, communicated through body language, such as unbroken eye contact. The hostile glare is difficult to confront, because the client can easily deny feeling angry and attempting to dominate. Videotaping sessions may help the counselor pinpoint examples of and give feedback on the nonverbal communication, but frequently the behavior occurs not in sessions but in impromptu encounters in the institutional routine, making it hard to capture on film. Peer review or feedback in groups may serve to validate a claim of intimidation, but only if the behavior is truly beyond the client's awareness. In many cases, clients are quite aware of their behavior, and continue it because it is successful. In these cases it is essential to find a low-threat, low-stress opportunity for both counselor and client to review the reasons for and the consequences of the intimidation. Counselors may want to schedule this discussion when support staff have been notified and are available at a moment's notice or at any sign of trouble.

Counselors will interpret the reasons for the intimidation depending on their theoretical frame of reference. Psychodynamic counselors may perceive the anger as the rage of an insecure child who has been denied adequate nurturing. Family systems counselors may view the anger as a pattern of competitive or symmetrical relationship. Cognitively-oriented therapists will look for underlying beliefs that lead to anger, such as that one should not be subjected to rules that apply to others; that one is innately superior to others; that life should be fairer or better than it is, etc.

Regardless of the counselor's explanation for the intimidation, a decision must be made whether to continue to work while feeling frightened or intimidated. When actual physical threats have been made, few counselors can effectively continue counseling. Subtle threats or intimidation are more difficult to reach a decision about because it is never easy to tell whether or not intimidation will remain psychological. Clients sometimes become angry to ward off queries into sensitive areas, but this rage is usually insufficient justification in and of itself to stop the counseling. In such cases counselors must assess their own willingness to persist, based on their level of commitment and tolerance for this type of behavior.

It is always better to feel safe or at least prepared in case of an emergency. Self-defense training can build confidence and thus reduce the feelings of panic that inhibit quick thinking in emergencies. Self-defense training will also teach the legal requirements and accepted techniques of restraint and use of minimal force. Calling early in a crisis for extra help is not a sign of weakness but a smart technique for keeping problems restricted. Good self-defense training designed for mental health workers will teach these skills.

In the institutional setting it is good practice to check up on clients by talking with security staff about their behavior on the ward or living unit. Clients often control their behavior for short sessions with the counselor, but act out around staff with lower status whom they see under the strain of day-to-day routine. But when sessions with the counselor become pressured, the facade of control can break down. The naive counselor is then caught unsuspecting.

Another good practice for counselors is to visit institutional clients in their living units outside of normal office hours. Behavior at these times often reveals interesting surprises about how clients relate to others in a group. Clients who present themselves as quiet and uninvolved during day hours may become a domineering force during night hours when treatment staff are normally gone. Clients who are "on their guard" during the day often become more "chatty" during the evening, as though the social rules of distance between staff and residents in institutions are suspended after five. An accurate assessment of clients may depend on these types of visits.

SUBSTANCE ABUSE COUNSELING

Substance abuse counselors frequently must decide what to do when a client is known to be violating laws or rules of the therapeutic program. Counselors need to figure out how much backsliding they can tolerate before terminating clients' treatment, whether they will work with clients presently high or drunk, and how to respond to the clients' inevitable attempts to get the counselor to condone or even join in the use and abuse of drugs and alcohol.

Especially in outpatient drug and alcohol counseling, policy should be established on what happens when clients come to sessions under the influence of drugs or alcohol. This policy should be clarified in advance. Counseling cannot be effective if the client is intoxicated, and many counselors send such clients home or call them a cab.

How counselors deal with such a touchy situation establishes their credibility with the client. The counselor cannot afford to overreact or underreact. Jokes or smiles of amusement are definitely inappropriate, as are insults or condemnations. It should be remembered that drugs and alcohol can reduce inhibitions and increase risk to the counselor. There should also be consideration of what to do about overdoses. Agency policy should be followed to the letter when dealing with these clients, who may be testing the limits of the program.

Counselors should also pay close attention to the ripple effect of a client's behavior. How does the incident affect communication between staff members? Does the client get special attention later for misbehavior? Are special alliances formed as people pair off to talk about the incident?

Substance abuse clients can be particularly resistant to counseling because they deny the seriousness of their problem and often become adept at manipulating people into overlooking or forgiving their problem behavior. These clients fascinate many counselors, and some drug and alcohol counselors become so immersed in the subculture of their clients that they begin to mirror their clients' behavior and values. It is important for these counselors to maintain social contacts with people uninvolved in the substance abuse treatment milieu. These contacts provide an anchor to the "straight" life and a less distorted mirror for counselors to see themselves clearly and notice undesirable changes that may occur as a result of intense exposure to drug and alcohol abuse.

There is no substitute for counselors knowing where they stand on the use of drugs and alcohol. Any uncertainty will eventually lead to compromising responses and ineffective, if not destructive, counseling.

DEALING WITH ANTISOCIAL CLIENTS

The question perhaps most frequently pondered when working with involuntary clients is whether there is a kind of client who cannot be counseled and who is totally unwilling to change. When faced with such clients, counselors frequently wonder whether they are giving up too soon, and they may criticize themselves for being too judgmental of their client.

A practical response to these concerns is that the average counselor working in public service has neither the training nor the legal authority to do what is necessary to stimulate change in clients such as a Hillside Strangler or a Son of Sam murderer. If these clients can benefit from therapy, it will be long-term, intensive work. Yochelson and Samenow's treatment approach as outlined in *The Criminal Personality* (1976, 1977) and Samenow's more recent discussion of that approach with juveniles in *Inside the Criminal Mind* (1984) is one method specifically developed for hardcore offenders. But by their own calculations their success rate was perhaps 20 or 30 percent. Moreover, most counselors will not have the authority to control the confinement or release of offenders and also will not have the luxury of investing fifteen to twenty hours a week with one small group of clients, as Yochelson and Samenow recommended. Modifications of their approach for less severely criminal clients is possible, but the problem of the most severe offender remains. Likewise, though some behavioral methods using aversive conditioning may be effective, the legal reality is that clients who don't want to subject themselves to such treatment can probably avoid it. Thus, some enticement must be offered to get clients active in treatment.

Fortunately, most people who are referred for treatment and who are involuntary clients are not as pathological as serial murderers. And involuntariness, like most human characteristics, is on a continuum from slight to severe. Most counselors will be referred clients who have serious problems to be sure, but problems that are amenable to a variety of counseling approaches, from transactional analysis to family therapy. The skills of the counselor, however, can be applied only if the client can be engaged in a counseling process. Some can, some can't. The counselor cannot help everyone and can waste energy trying to help those who choose not to change. Charlie Brown said it best: "No matter how hard you try, you can't throw a potato chip very far."

But a more venerable axiom also suggests that counselors sometimes may be responsible for much of clients' reluctance. It says, "You can chase a butterfly all day long; but only when you desist will it come to rest on your shoulder." Many clients just have to get sick and tired of being sick and tired before they will decide to change. Sometimes they have to be confined for awhile before they can face up to their predicament. The best the counselor may be able to do is to be there when the client finally asks for help. For noninstitutionalized involuntary clients, the counselor may be able to understand the effects of coercion enough to prevent the client's resentment from interfering with counseling. When this happens, the client's life becomes more open to cooperative examination and, therefore, successful counseling.

11

Conclusion

Chapter Eleven

The purpose of this book is not to recommend any particular approach for working with involuntary and resistant clients, but to talk generally about issues relevant to this work in a language that can be understood by counselors with many different frames of reference. When boiled down to their essence, the various frames of reference may not be substantially different anyway. Even behaviorists are likely these days to acknowledge the importance of counselors understanding themselves well enough not to get caught in emotional traps in counseling and, of course, psychoanalytic therapists have always emphasized the importance of so-called countertransference issues (Wachtel, 1984). The concepts discussed can be used by almost any therapist or counselor.

1. Counselors have to establish an environment in which communication can occur by looking at factors that facilitate and inhibit communication. Clients will not talk if they feel threatened and most are more likely to talk if they sense the counselor's understanding.
2. The client's problem must be identified. What needs changing? What does the client think needs changing, if anything? What is blocking the change? Are there reasons why adapting would not be in the client's interest? Do the client's underlying character and values block normal relationships, or is the person capable of being influenced by feedback about the effect of his behavior on others?
3. Particularly with involuntary clients, counselors must understand and respond to impediments to change that arise as a result of the client's involuntary entrance into the counseling process. Does the client trust the counselor or does he or she feel uncertain about disclosing information to the counselor? Does the client doubt the value of counseling? Is the client angry at the counselor because the counseling mandate was involuntary?
4. The counselor must select a counseling approach appealing to the style of the particular client. How does the client learn? Through action-oriented techniques? Through insight? Through talk about feelings? By seeing someone else perform the new behavior?
5. Counselors must understand the points at which their clients may be receptive to new understanding. What stage of treatment has the client reached? When should clients be confronted and when should they be allowed to "stew in their own juices?"
6. Counselors must develop an awareness of self and of organizational dynamics that hamper treatment. How can the counselor avoid inappropriate alliances with clients against other staff members? How can the counselor detect manipulation and respond therapeutically? What are the reasons the counselor has chosen to work with involuntary clients and do these reasons interfere with effectiveness?
7. Counselors must have some method to understand clients' tactics of resistance. How do clients evade personal responsibility by attacking or confusing the therapist? What is the best approach the counselor can use to respond effectively to these tactics from a particular client?

There is no magic wand to wave in counseling. Success is hard to measure, and some clients are hard to work with. Counseling involuntary clients has to be viewed both as a challenge and as an opportunity to hone one's counseling skills. But working with involuntary clients also gives an opportunity to develop a comprehensive view of human nature and a conception of morality or ethics. The involuntary client spurs us into thinking about our personal responsibilities and the nature of choice and free will. The presence of coercion requires that we examine our beliefs about human rights and the extent to which we wish to control the lives of others. The counselor values freedom, but also recognizes that there are responsibilities clients must recognize and assume. How to get clients to freely embrace their responsibilities is a paradox which may never be fully mastered.

BIBLIOGRAPHY

American Psychological Association. 1978. *Report of the task force on the role of psychology in the criminal justice system.* American Psychologist 33 (12): 160-165.

Anderson, C., and Stewart, S. *Mastering Resistance.* New York: Guilford Press, 1983.

Ansbacher, H. L. 1981. *Prescott Lecky's concept of resistance and his personality.* Journal of Clinical Psychology 37: 791-795.

Arcaya, J. 1978. *Coercive counseling and self-disclosure.* International Journal of Offender Therapy 22 (3): 231-237.

Basch, M. "Dynamic Psychotherapy and its Frustrations." In *Resistance: Psychodynamic and Behavioral Approaches,* edited by P. Wachtel. New York: Plenum Press, 1982.

Berman, E., and Segel, R. 1982. *The captive client: Dilemmas of psychotherapy in the psychiatric hospital.* Psychotherapy: Theory, Research, and Practice 19: 31-42.

Bernbaum, M. 1960. *Right to treatment.* American Bar Association Journal 56: 499.

Berne, E. *Games People Play.* New York: Grove Press, 1964.

Bowen, M. *Family Therapy in Clinical Practice.* New York: Jason Aronson, 1978.

Bratter, T. 1974. *Helping those who do not want to help themselves: A reality and confrontation orientation.* Corrective and Social Psychiatry & Journal of Behavior Technology, Methods, and Therapy 20 (4): 23-30.

Brehm, J. W. *A Theory of Psychological Reactance.* New York: Academic Press, 1966.

Brownell, A. 1981. *Counseling men through bodywork.* Personnel and Guidance Journal 60 (4): 252-255.

Collins, A. *The Lonely and Afraid: Counseling the Hard to Reach.* New York: Odyssey Press, 1969.

Corey, G., Corey, M., Callahan, P., and Russell, J. *Group Techniques.* Belmont, California: Wadsworth, Inc. 1982.

Duehn, W. D., and Proctor, E. K. 1977. *Initial client interaction and premature discontinuance in treatment.* American Journal of Orthopsychiatry 47: 284-290.

Dyer, W., and Vriend, J. 1973. *Counseling the reluctant client.* Journal of Counseling Psychology 20: 240-246.

Elkin, M. *Families Under the Influence.* New York: W. W. Norton, 1984.

Ellis, A. *Overcoming Resistance.* New York: Springer Publishing Company, 1985.

Enright, J., and Estep, R. 1973. *Metered counseling for the reluctant client.* Psychotherapy: Theory, Research, and Practice 10: 305-307.

Epperson, D. L., Bushway, D. J., and Warman, R. E. 1983. *Client self-terminations after one counseling session: Effects of problem recognition, counselor gender, and counselor experience.* Journal of Counseling Psychology 30: 307-315.

Erickson, M. "Resistant Patients." In *The Nature of Hypnosis and Suggestion,* vol. 1, edited by E. L. Rossi, 229-330. New York: Irvington Publishers, 1980.

Forest, G. *Confrontation in Psychotherapy of the Alchoholic.* Holmes Beach, Fla.: Learning Publications, Inc., 1982.

Fox, V. *Introduction to Corrections.* Englewood Cliffs, N.J.: Prentice-Hall, 1985.

Frankl, V. 1960. *Paradoxical intention: A logotherapeutic technique.* American Journal of Psychotherapy 14: 520-535.

Geiser, M., and Annitto, W. 1985. *Trafficking drug addicts: Some thoughts on the interchange between the criminal justice and mental health systems.* Paper presented at Annual Meeting of the Academy of Criminal Justice Sciences.

Gitterman, A. 1983. *Uses of resistance: A transactional view.* Social Work 28 (2): 127-131.

Glasser, W. *Reality Therapy.* New York: Harper and Row, 1965.

Goffman, E. *Asylums.* New York: Anchor Books, 1961.

Goodyear, R. K., and Bradley, F. O. 1980. *The helping process as contractual.* Personnel and Guidance Journal 58: 512-515.

Gordon, C., and Beresin, E. 1983. *Conflicting treatment models for the inpatient management of borderline patients.* American Journal of Psychiatry 140 (18): 979-983.

Gordon, R. *Interviewing: Strategies, Techniques, and Tactics.* 3d ed. Homewood, Ill.: Dorsey Press, 1980.

Gordon, T. *Parent Effectiveness Training.* New York: American Library, 1970.

Haley, J. *Strategies of Psychotherapy.* New York: Grune and Stratton, 1963.

Haley, J. *Uncommon Therapy: The Psychiatric Techniques of Milton Erickson.* New York: Norton, 1973.

Harris, G. 1984. *An interview with Stanton Samenow, coauthor of "The Criminal Personality."* Journal of Counseling and Development 63 (4): 227-229.

Harris, G., and Kirk, N. 1985. *A behavioral continuum: A look at the personality disorders.* Journal of Offender Counseling 6 (1): 2-8.

Harris, G., and Kirk, N. 1983. *A behavioral continuum: The need for an interdisciplinary approach.* Paper presented at Annual Meeting of the Academy of Criminal Justice Sciences.

Hartman, H. 1979. *Interviewing techniques in probation and parole.* Federal Probation 43: 55-62, 60-66.

Heitler, H. 1976. *Preparatory techniques in initiating expressive psychotherapy with lower-class, unsophisticated patients.* Psychological Bulletin 83: 339-352.

Ivey, A. *Intentional Interviewing and Counseling.* Monterey, Cal.: Brooks/Cole, 1983.

Johansen, K. 1983. The impact of patients with chronic character pathology on a hospital inpatient unit. Hospital and Community Psychiatry 34 (9): 842-846.

Kittrie, N. *The Right to be Different: Deviance Under Forced Therapy.* Baltimore: Johns Hopkins Press, 1971.

Kloss, J., and Karan, J. 1979. Community intervention for reluctant clients. Federal Probation 43: 37-43.

Korn, R., and McCorkle, L. *Criminology and Penology.* New York: Rinehart and Winston, 1959.

Kramer, S. 1985. *A systemwide approach to sex offender treatment and tracking.* Paper presented at Annual Meeting of the Academy of Criminal Justice Sciences.

Larke, J. 1985. Compulsory treatment: Some practical methods of treating the mandated client. Psychotherapy 22 (2): 262-268.

Larrabee, M. J. 1982. Working with reluctant clients through affirmation techniques. Personnel and Guidance Journal 61: 105-109.

Lasch, C. *The Culture of Narcissism: American Life in an Age of Diminishing Expectations.* New York: Norton, 1978.

Lazarus, A., and Fay, A. "Resistance or Rationalization." In *Resistance: Psychodynamic and Behavioral Approaches,* edited by P. Wachtel, 115-132. New York: Plenum Press, 1983.

Lion, J., and Reid, W., eds. *Assaults Within Psychiatric Facilities.* Orlando: Harcourt Brace Jovanovich, 1985.

May, R. *Love and Will.* New York: Dell Publishing, 1969.

McCarthy, B. R., and McCarthy, B. J. *Community-based Corrections.* Monterey, Cal.: Brooks/Cole, 1984.

Menninger, K. *The Crime of Punishment.* New York: The Viking Press, 1968.

Menninger, K. *Theory of Psychoanalytic Technique.* New York: Harper and Row, 1958.

Miller, W. 1985. Motivation for treatment: A review with special emphasis on alcoholism. Psychological Bulletin 98 (1): 84-107.

Monahan, J., ed. *Who is the Client? The Ethics of Psychological Intervention in the Criminal Justice System.* Washington, D.C.: American Psychological Association, 1980.

National Institute for Juvenile Justice and Delinquency Prevention. Office of Juvenile Justice and Delinquency Prevention. Law Enforcement Assistance Administration. U.S. Department of Justice. *Intervening with Convicted Serious Juvenile Offenders.* Washington, D.C.: GPO, 1983.

Palmer, S. E. 1983. Authority: An essential part of social work practice. Social Work Journal 28 (2): 120-125.

Paradise, L., and Wilder, D. 1979. The relationship between client and counseling effectiveness. Counselor Education and Supervision 19: 35-41.

Patterson, C. *Theories of Counseling and Personality.* New York: Harper and Row, 1980.

Peck, M. S. *People of the Lie.* New York: Simon and Schuster, 1983.

Pekarik, G. 1985. Coping with dropouts. Professional Psychology 16 (1): 114-123.

Pekarik, G. 1985. The effects of employing different termination criteria in dropout research. Psychotherapy 22: 86-91.

Pekarik, G., Jones, D., and Blodgett, C. 1986. Personality and demographics characteristics of dropouts and completers in a nonhospital residential alcohol treatment program. International Journal of the Addictions 21: 131-137.

Riché, M. 1979. Integrating families into a healing community: The use of structured and strategic family therapy in a psychodynamically-oriented hospital. Unpublished paper: Menninger Foundation.

Riordan, R. J., Matheny, K. B., and Harris, C. 1978. Helping counselors minimize client reluctance. Counselor Education and Supervision 18 (1): 14-22.

Ruppel, G., and Kaul, T. 1982. Investigation of social influence theory's conception of client resistance. Journal of Counseling Psychology 29: 305-307.

Russell, A. 1976. Limitations of family therapy. Clinical Social Work Journal 4: 83-92.

Samenow, S. *Inside the Criminal Mind.* New York: Times Books, 1984.

Shertzer, B., and Stone, S. *Fundamentals of Counseling.* Boston: Houghton Mifflin, 1974.

Solzhenitsyn, A. *One Day in the Life of Ivan Denisovich.* New York: Bantam Books, 1963.

Strean, H. *Resolving Resistances in Psychotherapy.* New York: John Wiley, 1985.

Teismann, M. 1980. Convening strategies in family therapy. Family Progress 19: 373-400.

Tennen, H., Rohrbaugh, M., Press, S., and White, L. 1981. Reactance theory and therapeutic paradox: A compliance/defiance model. Psychotherapy: Theory, Research, and Practice 18 (1): 14-22.

Van Hoose, W. H., and Kottler, J. A. *Ethical Issues in Counseling and Psychotherapy.* San Francisco: Jossey-Bass, 1985.

Vanier, J. *Man and Woman He Made Them.* Mahwah, N.J.: Paulist Press, 1985.

Varga, L. 1971. Motivational intervention: Theoretical considerations in employment counseling. Journal of Employment Counseling 8 (3): 137-144.

Vontress, C. 1974. Barriers in cross-cultural counseling. Counseling and Values 18 (3): 160-165.

Ward, D. 1984. Termination of individual counseling. Journal of Counseling and Development 63 (1): 21-26.

Watzlawick, P., Beavin, J., and Jackson, D. *Pragmatics of Human Communication.* New York: Norton, 1967.

Watzlawick, P., Weakland, J. H., and Fisch, R. *Change: Principles of Problem Formation and Problem Resolution.* New York: Norton, 1974.

West, M. 1975. Building a relationship with the unmotivated client. Psychotherapy: Theory, Research, and Practice 12: 48-51.

Yochelson, S., and Samenow, S. *The Criminal Personality: Profile for Change.* New York: Jason Aronson, 1976.

Yochelson, S., and Samenow, S. *The Criminal Personality: The Change Process.* New York: Jason Aronson, 1977.